Park City Walking Guide

2nd Edition

By Beverly Hurwitz MD

Surrogate Press®

ALSO BY BEVERLY HURWITZ
Park City Hiking Guide
Nobody Else's Business - A Novel
Is the Cat Lady Crazy? - A Novel

Published in the United States by
Surrogate Press®
Park City, Utah
an imprint of Faceted Press®
Surrogate Press, LLC
SurrogatePress.com

ISBN: 978-1-947459-51-9

Library of Congress Control Number: 2020922747

Book cover design by: Beverly Hurwitz

Interior design by: Katie Mullaly, Surrogate Press®

Photography by the author except where noted otherwise.

Table of Contents

Pandemically Speaking

At the time this book was being updated in the life-changing year of 2020, the future was uncertain and there were no indicators that the resort town of Park City would soon get back to normal. Still, this book was written with the hopes that people will ultimately be able to safely resume socialization and travel. In the meantime, Park City walks have been impacted by COVID-19 in two major ways.

On the positive side, many more people have taken up walking for exercise and recreation. This became apparent as soon as the ski resorts abruptly closed on March 15, 2020, and indoor exercise facilities lost their appeal. Park City's paths and trails became busier than normal, which can make **neighborhood walks** preferable to cyclist-dominated trails at peak times. This book includes routes through several Park City neighborhoods.

Unfortunately, the pandemic has also resulted in a significant reduction of Park City's **free public bus service** that enables walkers to get to preferred terrain. A blue bag over a bus stop sign indicates the stop isn't currently served. Seek current information about Park City's bus service at *go.parkcity.org/InfoPoint/* or *parkcity.org/departments/transit-bus*.

Driving to trailheads can be problematic because **parking is limited,** and development keeps devouring what little is left. Paid parking will probably become the norm as demand grows and open land shrinks. Also, you never want to park in an unauthorized place, not even for a few minutes. The **risk of getting towed is high** and **so is the cost**.

You could walk to your destination. Having a friend or a driver service drop you off is another option. Hopefully, bus service will be restored and the bus instructions for these walks will be viable if not the most convenient way to get there, once the pandemic is behind us.

Historically, Park City was an early **hotspot** for COVID-19, probably because it hosts visitors from around the world. There's speculation that the corona virus had already arrived in Park City in January 2020, when Sundance Film Festival attendees with fevers were testing negative for influenza. COVID in the USA hadn't yet been recognized, and those who suffered the symptoms called their illness the "Festival Flu." My husband and I contracted COVID-19 in early March. My husband spent three weeks on a ventilator and miraculously survived. Eight months later, neither of has completely recovered from this vicious virus.

A mask mandate in Summit County reduced the incidence of COVID over the summer, but as I am writing this in late 2020, the incidence of infection is rapidly rising. Whether you live here or are visiting, please follow guidelines for **mask wearing, hand washing**, and **social distancing**. The life you save may be your own or someone dear to you.

Hopefully, the next time I update this book, information regarding the pandemic will not need to be included.

Why Walk

Park City's reputation as a haven for skiers, cyclists, shoppers and film lovers overshadows the fact that it's wonderful place to get out of the car and just go for a walk.

This book will guide you along **paved paths** and roads in and around the variety of **neighborhoods** that comprise this spectacular mountain community. Some easy off-road **trails** are included to whet appetites for hiking.

Each of these walks exposes you to Park City's **colorful history** and/or its **diverse ecology**. Hopefully, this book will also inspire you to become a walker if you aren't one already. The benefits of regular walking are plentiful and profound.

For starters, walking is the **most natural, safest**, and most readily **available** form of human exercise. Walking can be accomplished almost **anywhere, anytime**, even if you only have a few minutes or are stuck in an airport.

Regular walking **improves fitness, health, weight control, sleep, mood, and longevity**. Walking can be therapeutic for a wide variety of medical problems.

Walking **improves cognition**. Some of history's most revered thinkers, such as Plato, Aristotle, and Thomas Jefferson were avid walkers, and are said to have done their best thinking while walking. New research is showing that "greener" schools that expose children to nature, are reporting that their students show improvements in problem solving, critical thinking, leadership, teamwork and resilience, and they score higher on standardized tests.

Walking with a friend or family member can **strengthen relationships**.

Walking can provide **solitude** or private time for those who need to de-stress, solve problems, make decisions or get their creative juices percolating.

Walkers can **get to places** where other travelers cannot go, not even on a bicycle

Walking is **free**. **No training** or **special equipment** is needed. Your shoes won't be stolen while you stop for lunch. Your walking gear can be your everyday, everywhere gear.

Walking outdoors is a **sensory awakening**. A walker can see, hear, smell and touch things that motorists, cyclists and runners miss when they whiz by.

Regular walkers gain **appreciation of community** not experienced by other travelers. Many successful politicians start their careers by walking around.

Walking around is considered to be an important strategy for **success in business** management and leadership.

With discretion, walking can be **combined** with numerous other activates.

Imagine what a **healthier environment** you could live in if auto traffic was reduced because people embraced walking as transportation.

Your **kids** and **dog** could benefit too.

You will be astounded by how **easy**, invigorating, stimulating, and entertaining walking can be. Alternatively, if you're seeking challenge, **walking can be as hard as you care to make it.**

For walkers who want to get more into the mountains, my second book, *Park City Hiking Guide* provides maps and directions for 45 hikes in and around Park City's more rugged terrain, along with valuable information about altitude fitness, hiking gear, and how to manage emergencies ranging from earthquakes to rattlesnakes. This paperback facilitates navigation of Park City's complex trail system with its many twists and turns. (*Park City Hiking Guide* is available in a variety of Park City stores and on-line by major booksellers).

PARK CITY HIKING GUIDE

Beverly Hurwitz MD

The book you're now reading, *Park City Walking Guide,* was originally researched in 2014 and published in 2017 (under the title *A Walker's Guide To Park City*). To keep up with the changes of the rapidly developing Park City community, this book was updated, retitled and republished in 2021.

Happy walking!

About Park City

Just off Interstate Route 80 as it streams from New York City to San Francisco, the town of Park City sits on about 17.5 square miles (45.5 km²) of mountain terrain, 7,000 feet (2,133 m) above sea level. Its official address is Summit County, Utah, U.S.A.

The mountains of Park City are part of the Wasatch Range at the western edge of the **Rocky Mountains**. The view in this photo shows the **Wasatch Mountains** as seen from the Salt Lake Valley. A few thousand feet shorter than the Colorado Rockies, the Wasatch Mountains stretch for about 160 miles (257 km) from Idaho to central Utah. They form the eastern edge of the **Great Basin** where an ancient ocean once occupied the American southwest. The **Great Salt Lake** and **Bonneville Salt Flats** are remnants of that ocean.

Park City is said to be located along the **Wasatch Back**, while the Salt Lake Valley is referred to as the **Wasatch Front**. "Wasatch" in Native American languages means "mountain pass," or "low mountains," or "low place in high mountains." As a low place in high mountains, Park City became the route of the **Lincoln Highway**, America's first transcontinental thoroughfare and now Interstate Route 80.

The town of Park City, commonly called **Old Town**, occupies a narrow canyon that spills out of the mountains from the even narrower Ontario and Empire Canyons to the south, as seen in this photo. This view looks west toward more mountains and canyons.

Park City's suburbs and the **Snyderville Basin** are located on a mountain plateau to the north and east. Also east of Park City, there's explosive development going on around the **Jordanelle Reservoir** and throughout the **Heber Valley**.

Like other famous mountain resorts in the western USA, Park City developed in the middle of the nineteenth century as a **mining town** and evolved into a **ski town** in the last half of the twentieth century. To control the burgeoning growth of recent decades, residents and their leaders have worked hard and taxed themselves to preserve both the town's historic character and open space. Numerous Park City addresses are on multiple historic registries and there are about **7,000 acres of preserved open space** and more than **400 miles (644+ km) of maintained trails** in and around the town. In fact, there are many more miles of trails than roads.

The 2010 **census** counted about 7,500 residents living in approximately 2,900 households, with males outnumbering females by about 112 to 100. Approximately **70%** of Park City residences are **second homes** whose owners are not counted in the census. In 2020, there were about 5,000 students enrolled in the Park City public school district and about another thousand or so attending nine private schools and preschools. Due to the area's rapid growth, these statistics may dramatically change with the 2020 census.

Park City is one of the **wealthiest** small towns in the United States. Providing an easier commute to the state capital than do many locations along the Wasatch Front, it serves as a bedroom community for the growing Salt Lake City metropolis. In addition to **tourism, retail**, and **service** industries, several **manufacturing** companies provide local employment. Park City's ease of access to an **international airport** is ideal for traveling executives. **Farming** and **ranching** are important occupations in surrounding Summit and Wasatch Counties.

The number of residents who live in Park City is greatly exceeded by the number of tourists who visit. Retirees from Phoenix, Las Vegas, Texas and other hot climates lease **skier housing** in the summer to enjoy the cool mountain temperatures. Salt Lakers regularly come for skiing, cycling, concerts and events, and to escape summer heat and valley inversions in winter.

It's estimated that Park City attracts more than **three million visitors** annually and that number was rapidly rising prior to the COVID pandemic. Once tourists discover that this recreational paradise is less than an hour from an international airport, they come back and send friends. Most come in winter, but summer is almost as popular. Locals often say they moved here for the winters, but they stay forever because summers are so spectacular. There are fewer visitors in spring and autumn, but no matter the season, all but a few of the walks in this book can be enjoyed without crowds.

Additional **information about Park City** is found in the next three chapters.

Mountain Town Amenities

While Park City's mountains are a magnet for many, this little town also offers mountains of entertainment, eats, education, and enterprise.

ENTERTAINMENT

Film is a prime Park City attraction. Find **theaters** at the Holiday Village Shopping Mall north of Old Town, at the Jim Santy auditorium in the old Park Avenue high school, and in the Redstone area in Kimball Junction. Check for outdoor screenings in summer. Select films are sponsored by *parkcityfilm.org.* Park City is also the home of a fledgling movie studio.

During the **Sundance Film Festival**, (*www.sundance.org*), which is accompanied by other film festivals, big rooms all over town become movie-houses. Visitors who score lodging during Sundance, might find that the gym or house of worship they planned to attend has been transformed into a theater.

The **Egyptian Theatre** on Main Street, (*egyptiantheatercompany.org*) and **The Eccles Theater** at the Park City High School, host live theater, comedy, music, dance, and other entertainment.

Park City is a mecca for live **music**. The nonprofit organization, **Mountain Town Stages**, (*mountaintownmusic.org*) has been known to arrange **200+**

community concerts a year. It also provides outreach programs in schools and assists musicians with networking. You can also find public **sound gardens** and community **pianos.**

Outdoor **concerts** may be staged at the ski resorts, the Dejoria Center in nearby Kamas, and other locations. Some are free of charge. The **Park City Institute,** (*parkcityinstitute.org*)*,* and other entities sponsor concerts by nationally recognized musicians.

Entertainment may also be found in restaurants, nightclubs and the hotels. **Main Street** traditionally hosts holiday parades, street markets and other special events.

Winter entertainment might include athlete and celebrity **ski races** and watching skiers and boarders fly through the **half-pipe** in competition. Spectators can also watch aerialists train and compete at the **Utah Olympic Park** in Kimball Junction year-round.

Artists and **photographers** also abound in Park City. Numerous galleries bedazzle with unique creations and stunning images of mountain scenery and wildlife. Learn about **free gallery tours** of the historic district at *parkcitygalleryassociation.com*.

Local painters and sculptors have decorated some of Park City's trails and tunnels. Spruced-up moose around town display Park City's love of **public art**.

The nonprofit **Kimball Art Center**, (*kimballartcenter.org*), sponsors exhibits, classes and workshops for artists, an annual arts festival in August and other activities.

EATS

A tally from before the COVID pandemic counted some **180 restaurants** in and around Park City. Ranging from pricey fine dining on Main Street to budget eateries in the suburbs, choices are diverse and plentiful. Utah seems to attract entrepreneurial young chefs and the Salt Lake and Heber Valleys also offer tasty options.

Artisan bakers, cheese makers, brewers, distillers, chocolatiers and other **food crafters** are choosing to locate in and around Park City. Along with multiple supermarkets, find farm stands and boutique groceries and bakeries. Though gardening at altitude has its challenges, **community gardening** is a "growing" trend.

Beyond Park City and the Wasatch Front, Utah is largely **agrarian**. Beef, hogs, lambs, turkeys, eggs and dairy products come from Utah. There's an **aquaculture** industry and you'll find Utah trout on many menus. Utah crops include apples, cherries, peaches, raspberries, onions, potatoes and dry beans. Calling itself the "beehive state", Utah is known for its honey.

You can drink alcoholic beverages in Utah, but as in some other states, spirits by the bottle are only sold in state-controlled liquor stores, closed on Sundays and holidays, (including Pioneer Day on July 24). Licensed restaurants and bars can serve alcohol to patrons over age 21. Grocery and convenience stores can sell 4% beer.

It's illegal to transport alcoholic beverages into Utah from other locations. **Driving** in Utah with a blood alcohol level of **0.05%** is also **illegal.** If you do drink alcohol, remember that Park City has a free transportation system in addition to multiple driver services. It's also very **walkable**. You can party here and stay safe. Additional information about getting a drink in Utah may be found at *visitsaltlake.com/restaurants-and-bars/drinking-in-utah/*.

EDUCATION

Intriguing exhibits at the **Park City Museum** on Main Street, (*parkcityhistory.org*), capture the town's vibrant history and evolution. Research resources are also available for those who wish to know more.

A museum and environmental education are featured at the **Swaner Preserve** and **Ecocenter** of Utah State University in the Snyderville Basin, (*swanerecocenter.org*).

Learn about skiing history at the **Alf Engen Ski Museum** and the **George Eccles 2002 Olympic Winter Games Museum** in Olympic Park, (*engenmuseum.org*).

Park City citizens support a state-of-the-art **municipal library** in Old Town, a local branch of the **county library** in Kimball Junction, and book exchange programs. Educational films, TED talks and similar events are sponsored by local nonprofits.

In addition to a **highly rated public-school system**, Park City offers several private schools including an alternative high school for youths competing in winter sports.

Park City also has its own cooking and wine schools, and of course: ski schools, fly-fishing schools, golf schools, SUP schools, cycling schools, horseback riding schools, and just about any other kind of expert instruction you might be interested in.

ENTERPRISE

The tiny town of Park City has its own newspaper, radio station and TV station. The **Park Record newspaper** is published twice a week and also provides online news and information at *parkrecord.com*.

The **radio station, KPCW**, provides local news and programming daily and can be found on the FM dial at 91.7, and on-line at *kpcw.org*. Park City's **television station, PCTV**, provides on-line programming at *parkcity.tv*.

Park City is a treasure trove of world-class luxury **resorts** clustered around the ski areas. **Lodging options** range from opulent hotels, houses and condos, to dormitory facilities and an RV campground. Camping options are available nearby.

Lavish **spa** facilities are offered by local hotels, while independent spas, **gyms,** and **yoga studios** also abound. In addition to private and municipal work-out facilities, there are public **skate** and **dirt bike parks**. Seasonally, **electric bikes** are available for a nominal rental fee.

In 2019, The **Woodward Center** opened up along Park City's highway entrance to provide training options for extreme athletes. The **National Ability Center** in Park City sponsors athletic and recreational opportunities for individuals with disabilities.

In addition to having a hospital, urgent care clinics, and private medical and alternative **health care** practices, expertise in joint regeneration and repair in Park City, (home of the U.S. Ski Team), is an attraction for serious and professional athletes.

Shopping is also a Park City attraction. In addition to some popular chain stores, Main Street features unique boutiques and galleries. If the moose mugs you purchased won't fit in your suitcase, some Main Street merchants will ship your purchase for you. There's also a multitude of sporting goods stores and **The Outlets Park City** in Kimball Junction provides an outdoor mall with a playground.

Unique second-hand treasures can be found at the nonprofit **Park City Recycling Center,** *(recycleutah.org)*, at the **Christian Center of Park City,** *(ccofpc.org)*, which supports community services, at the **Park City ReStore,** *(habitat-utah.org/restore)*, which supports Habitat for Humanity, and in **local consignment shops.**

Then, besides the cross-country and downhill skiing and snowboarding, there's also snowshoeing, snow tubing, snowmobiling, snow cycling (on bikes with snow tires), dogsled and horse sleigh riding, ice-skating, curling, hockey, in-line skating, golf, tennis, pickleball, horseback riding, cycling and electric cycling, hiking, swimming, sailing, stand-up paddle boarding, balloon riding and kite-flying. And, if none of that seems appealing, neighboring communities offer fly-fishing, river running, rock climbing, **state parks, national parks,** and really special activities like riding in a horse-drawn wagon through an elk herd *(https://wildlife.utah.gov/discover/hardware-ranch.html)*.

And finally, **Park City is a great place for walkers**. Park City and its surrounds are connected by an **extensive trail** system, a **free public transportation** system, and an **aerial-transport** system that makes mountain terrain readily accessible. For those uninclined to walk on dusty trails, a variety of neighborhoods provide easy or invigorating and entertaining, paved walking routes. You don't have to be an athlete to enjoy Park City's mountains and the many amenities they inspire.

Park City's Colorful Past

Long before Park City's existence, humans inhabited the **Great Basin** region of the southwest United States, living as nomadic hunters and gatherers in extended family groups. They followed game herds and ripening plants, and produced tools made of bones, stones and wood.

The **Fremont** culture existed in Utah, north of the Colorado River, from about AD 1 to AD 1300. Unlike hunter/gatherers, these people depended on **agriculture** and lived in pit houses, structures built partially into the ground. They farmed corn, squash and beans, and produced **pottery** and **basketry**. It's not known if the Fremont migrated away due to drought, transitioned back to a hunter-gatherer existence, or blended with other tribes, but their unique cultural signature faded away after AD 1300.

Droughts and short growing seasons probably motivated early **migrations**. There's evidence of a 30-year drought in the southwest United States starting about AD 1270, when **Shoshonean (Numic)** speaking people had come to occupy northern and eastern Utah. Their primary activities were hunting, gathering, and seasonal rounds of travel and trade.

After **horses** and material goods were introduced to Native Americans by **Spanish explorers** in the late 1600s, the Shoshoneans became more mobile and expanded their terrain and trading routes. Ultimately, the **Northern Shoshone, Goshute (Western Shoshone), Southern Paiute,** and the **Ute** tribes came to call Utah home.

Utah **Native Americans** had a family-centered culture with great reverence for grandparents and women. They lived in groups of about 200 persons, scattered geographically to conserve game and plant food sources. Spanish colonial administrators didn't control the Shoshonean tribes like they did the **Pueblo** tribes to the south, but intruders started to change the way of life of Utah's Native Americans in the 1820s, when the **Santa Fe Trail** from Missouri to New Mexico brought increasing numbers of trappers and traders northwards into Utah.

When the **Mormon pioneers** with their handcarts and covered wagons arrived in 1847, several Native Americans tribes were living along the Wasatch Front. Conflict arose when Mormon settlements infringed on tribal farmland, fishing and hunting grounds. Less than two decades after the Mormons arrived, a federal agent advised **President Abraham Lincoln** (1861-65), that the tribes had been driven into nakedness and famine. Only when they were starving and freezing did these peaceful indigenous people resort to raids and theft of livestock. In response, Utah's new settlers, who outnumbered the native people, demanded that the federal government intervene. (In 1830, Congress had passed the **Indian Removal Act**, empowering the U.S. government to forcibly remove Native Americans away from populations of European settlers.)

Ultimately, tribal lands were reduced to **reservations**. Most Native Americans do not live on reservations, but currently, they comprise less than one percent of the population of Summit County which formerly belonged to their ancestors.

Park City's more recent history tells the story of a little nineteenth-century mountain mining camp that became one of the most popular resort destinations in the world.

Early 1800s: Native Americans, trappers and traders frequently traveled through the mountain pass that borders Park City. On their way to Salt Lake City in 1847, the Mormon pioneers traveled through **Emigration Canyon**, a nearby Wasatch Mountains pass.

In **1848**, entrepreneur Parley P. Pratt explored the canyon between Salt Lake City and the future Park City. Mormon leader **Brigham Young** gave Pratt the canyon, through which he promptly built a toll road in order to collect fees from travelers lured west by the **California Gold Rush** (1848-1855). This "Golden Pass" also provided a thoroughfare for stagecoaches and mail. Today **Parley's Canyon** is the route of one of America's major highways, Interstate Route 80.

1850s: Utah was organized as an incorporated **territory** of the United States by an 1850 act of Congress. It wouldn't become the **45th state** of the Union until 1896, after the Mormon practice of polygamy was officially renounced. (Polygamy is still practiced by fundamentalist groups throughout North America.)

Several families migrated up Parley's Canyon in the early 1850s to homestead on the mountain plateau (basin) just north of future Park City. Grassy meadows with abundant streams enabled the settlers to graze animals and grow food. (In 1862, Congress passed the first of the **Homestead Acts** which ultimately gave ten percent of America's land away to homesteaders).

Amongst the first settlers were George and Rhoda Snyder. There was also a Samuel Comstock Snyder who opened a lumber mill. The basin came to be called **Snyderville** and **Snyder's Mill** is now one of its subdivisions.

1860s: William Kimball began operating a **stagecoach**, improving transportation through Parley's Canyon. Today **Kimball Junction** is the commercial center of suburban Park City.

During the **Civil War** (1861-1865), President Abraham Lincoln was concerned that the Utah settlers, like the Confederate states, might try to secede. He sent Union soldiers to monitor the settlers and protect federal mail routes. Some of these soldiers had been prospectors during the California Gold Rush and they spent their leisure time looking for **precious metals** in the local mountains. Their searches lead to the **discovery** of rich veins of **silver** ore, as well as lead, zinc and gold.

News of the finds traveled quickly, seducing adventurers from diverse backgrounds to come seek their fortunes. At the same time, Mormon leader Brigham Young spurned the lure of precious metals and forbade his followers to prospect for any commodity other than **coal.** His plan for economic growth was agriculture.

Today, Park City's neighborhoods with names like **Silver Springs**, **Silver Summit, Silver Creek**, etc., commemorate the importance of silver to the area. Twenty-five miles north of Park City, Mormon coal prospectors settled the small town of **Coalville**, and made it the seat of county government, to "rule over" the unruly mining camp to its south.

In 1869, the USA was physically united by the completion of the **Transcontinental Railroad** in Promontory Point, Utah.

1870s: First settlers George and Rhoda Snyder named the area Parley's Park City. With its name quickly abbreviated, the tiny town of Park City was born into America's **Gilded Age**. American author **Mark Twain** termed the period from the 1870s to about 1900 the "Gilded Age", because there seemed to be a thin golden veneer (gilding) covering over a morass of social problems and injustice.

In Park City, the mines would ultimately create **23 millionaire mine owners**, while legions of laborers toiled in cold, wet, dark, poorly ventilated mine tunnels with rocks falling on their heads, while breathing in mold and toxic dust, for ten hours every day except Independence Day and Christmas.

Construction of the Transcontinental Railroad had required the labor of thousands of strong backs, but the Civil War had killed and maimed many young men and there was a nationwide shortage of workers, especially in the sparsely populated west. The need for laborers, and the fact that skilled workers could earn more in America than in troubled homelands, sparked the **emigration of an estimated ten million Europeans and Asians** to the United States during the Gilded Age.

Most of the European immigrants in this era came from the harsh climate of Northern Europe. The railroads were the major employer, but opportunities were also abundant in factories, mining, farming, finance, and most other trades and occupations.

Upon completion of the railroad, many immigrant laborers who had worked on the western tracks looked to the **mining industry** for jobs, and hundreds came to prospect or seek employment in Park City. Prospectors often set up camps around their claims. The posh midsection of Deer Valley Resort, now called **Silver Lake**, was once the location of the first mining camp, called Lake Flat.

Park City's early settlers proved to have a civic spirit and they established a **free public school in 1875**. It provided instruction for both children and adults, including immigrants and illiterate laborers who had never previously had access to formal education.

In the latter part of the decade, the **Ontario Mine** became one of the world's leading silver producers.

1880s: Early in this decade, **railroad spur lines** were completed from Coalville to both Kimball Junction and Park City. To keep building tracks, trees were felled at great rates and some skilled lumberjacks, called "tie hacks", could fabricate railroad ties right where the trees were chopped down.

Coal from the mines of Coalville powered the railroad steam engines, providing the high capacity transport needed to make **large-scale mining** profitable. The days of using horses to pull wagons full of heavy rocks were

RAILS EAST TO PROMONTORY
THE UTAH STATIONS

Aaron S. Raymond   Richard E. Fike

1981

CULTURAL RESOURCE SERIES
No. 8

ending, (though horses would continue to haul logs out of the forest until they were replaced by gasoline engines in the 1920s.)

Expansion of the railroads enabled transport of bigger and better equipment to improve mine productivity. Mines such as the Mayflower, Woodside, Crescent, and numerous others arose to compete with the Ontario. Mine expansion fueled growth of the town, resulting in Park City being legally incorporated in 1884.

Expansion of the railroads also brought more laborers to Park City, and **expansion of the mines** lured destitute workers away from depleted mines in Scotland, Ireland, Scandinavia and other locales. Cornish miners from the southern tip of England (Cornwall) were especially valued for their hard rock engineering skills.

Also present were many Chinese laborers. Due to hardship in China and economic opportunity promised by the California Gold Rush, and then by railroad construction, many Chinese men had immigrated to California and the western U.S. during the previous two decades. Even little old Park City had a **Chinatown**, located where the China Bridge parking structure now stands on the east side of "Swede Alley."

Chinese immigrants were appreciated for being especially skilled, eager workers. They were particularly adept at dangerous jobs involving explosives, essential to railroad construction, but their willingness to work for lower wages, along with the foreignness of their language and customs, generated widespread resentment of these immigrants. Chinese job seekers were not hired as miners in Park City but became cooks and launderers and filled positions that others wouldn't. The so-called **China Bridge** was built in Park City so that Caucasians could walk over instead of through the neighborhood where the Chinese resided.

Ultimately, Chinese workers were blamed for unemployment in other populations, prompting the federal government under **President Chester A. Arthur** (1881-85) to pass the **Chinese Exclusion Act** of 1882, greatly restricting Chinese immigration to the United States. In 1886, the *Park Record* newspaper proclaimed the "Chinese must go."

(The Chinese Exclusion Act was repealed in 1943 when China became an American ally against Imperial Japan, but Chinese immigration to the USA remained severely restricted until the **Immigration Act** of 1965.)

Also in the 1880s, **engineering technology** in the mining industry reached new heights and depths. An enormous "Cornish" Pump (as illustrated here) was transported from Philadelphia to Park City by freight train for the purpose of removing water from constantly flooded mine tunnels. This device could

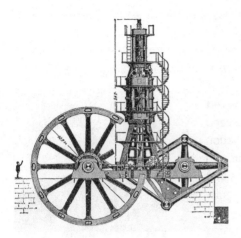

extract four million gallons (15 million L) of water a day from a thousand feet (305 m) below ground. However, as the mining tunnels reached deeper levels, engineers such as John Keetley developed giant drainage tunnels under the mountains to get rid of the water. It took laborers about six years of working day and night to build the 5-mile (8 km) long **Keetley Drain Tunnel**, 1,500 feet (457+ m) below ground, and its two ends met exactly in the middle as planned. Today, the **Keetley** and **Spiro** Drain Tunnels provide some of Park City's municipal water.

By the mid-1880s the need for lumber for both fuel and construction had ravaged forests on Park City's mountainsides. Then, without trees to stop snow and wet soil from sliding down steep inclines, winter **avalanches** and spring **mudslides** destroyed some mining camps. Eighty-four people died in avalanches in Ontario Canyon one snowy winter. That prompted many miners to move out of the mountains and into the growing town.

In 1889, flourishing Park City became one of the first localities in Utah to have **electric light**. Candles, oil lamps, and the many fires they started were on the wane.

1890s: A rail line between Park City and Salt Lake City was completed, facilitating travel as well as the transport of silver ore to a large **smelter** in Salt Lake City. The process of smelting (roasting) rocks to remove precious metals, dates back about 2,700 years, when humans first learned how to get the lead out.

In spite of some economic downturn during this decade, Park City mines continued to be productive and the **Silver King Mine** became another industry giant. Its mill near the Bonanza chairlift on Park City Mountain, separated rocks containing precious metals from useless rock, reducing the cost of transporting heavy ore to a smelter.

In 1898, a **Great Fire** of uncertain cause incinerated about 200 Park City businesses and residences, leaving some 500 people homeless. Chinatown was obliterated and never recovered, but profits from the mines, charitable contributions, and the determination of the citizens resulted in prompt reconstruction. As you walk through Old Town Park City today, notice that many buildings show architectural features that were fashionable at the turn of the nineteenth century.

1900s: This decade gave birth to aviation, the Model-T automobile, the New York City subway system, Freud's theories on sexuality, silent movies, and the first baseball World Series

In 1901, **Theodore (Teddy) Roosevelt (TR)** became the youngest man to ascend to the presidency upon the assassination of **President William McKinley**. Through 1909, TR propelled the United States into a **Progressive Era** by pursuing regulation of the railroads, foods and drugs, by breaking up big trusts, and by promising fairness for all citizens.

Originally from New York City, TR had worked as a rancher in the Dakotas and authored several nature books. As president, he made **conservation of natural resources** a priority, establishing some of the first national parks, forests and monuments, of which the state of Utah has an especially generous share.

Park City's mines continued to profit in the 1900s but also experienced tragedy when an explosion in the **Daly West Mine** killed 34 miners in 1902, just as the city was recovering from the Great Fire.

The 30-mile trip to a Salt Lake City hospital had been a hardship for injured miners, especially in winter. Soon after the catastrophe, social and fraternal organizations, private citizens, and the local miners' labor union all came together to raise funds and build the **Miner's Hospital in Park City**, completed in 1904.

Legends about the ghosts of deceased miners are often heard in old mining towns. In Park City such ghosts came to be called **"Tommy Knockers,"** and some locals claim to have seen a ghost in a yellow slicker in the Miner's Hospital. Should you actually hear thuds in the earth while walking about here, it is more likely due to settling of the ground within the hundreds of miles of tunnels that the miners blasted through these mountains, than due to paranormal phenomena.

19-Teens: Main events of this decade were **World War One** (1914-1918), and the opening of the Panama Canal. After 2,000 years of Imperial Rule, the Emperor of China was forced to abdicate, and the Russian Revolution overthrew 300 years of rule by the Romanov Dynasty. Stainless steel was invented, and Ford Motor Company introduced the assembly line. In New York City, 25,000 women marched up Fifth Avenue to demand the right to vote.

Back in Park City during this decade, a legendary Park City woman named Rachel Urban, along with her husband George, operated sixteen houses of **prostitution** (called cribs) on what are now Heber Avenue and Deer Valley Drive. One house featured a bar and a piano player. The rest of the cribs were single rooms. The neighborhood was called "The Row", "The Line", and the "Red Light District," a term that probably originated because railroad workers, who carried red lanterns at night, left them outside crib doors to show they were in use.

Single women were scarce in Park City's early days and for many single miners, cribs, saloons, and occasional community dances were the only available places to enjoy female companionship. In the 1800s, miners had been required by federal law to live in **boarding houses** provided by the mine operators. Even after this law was repealed in 1901, for many of these young men, boarding houses with restrictive rules were still the only available housing.

Rachel Urban was the Madam of "The Row". She's been described as a physically enormous woman with a wooden leg. She was said to have birthed six children, only one of whom survived, and to have kept a cussing parrot on her parlor porch.

Rachel came to be called **Mother Urban** because she took exceptionally good care of her employees, who in turn took good care of the town's laborers and millionaires. She had a physician provide regular check-ups for her workers, threw Christmas parties for single miners, and helped the illiterate to write letters home. She paid substantial fines and taxes for her business and properties and was a welcome contributor to the city's coffers. It's also said that she provided financial assistance to Park City's needy, discretely coming to their doors after dark to protect their privacy.

Rachel Urban died in 1933, and a popular jazz club called Mother Urban's Rathskeller operated on Heber Avenue until 2005.

Another successful Park City Madam was Bessie Wheeler, who reportedly took derelicts off the street to rehabilitate them, cared for sick miners, and sent Christmas money to needy families. Stories about these madams left this author wondering if entrepreneurial, philanthropic women of this era had so few opportunities, that prostitution was the most accessible profession by which they could earn enough to fulfill their missions of helping others.

Although prostitution was a thriving quasi-legal industry in Park City from the 1870s through the 1950s, it wasn't always legal to operate a saloon. A **temperance movement** had been growing around the country since the 1840s, especially in the western United States where there was much religious piety. Utah was one of 33 states to ban the manufacture and distribution of alcohol (1917), even before the United States Congress did the same with the **National Prohibition (Volstead) Act** of 1919, and the Eighteenth Amendment to the U.S. Constitution in 1920.

Illegal stills came into existence as soon as prohibition did, especially in big cities and western mining towns. Those who labored in the mines had few remedies to relieve the pain and drudgery of their physical toil. The average lifespan of a miner wasn't much more than forty years. Their pay was a few dollars a day and they had no health benefits, just enormous health risks. Smoking opium was another way some relieved their pain, until the **Harrison Act** outlawed opium in 1914.

(Prohibition of alcohol was a dismal failure that spawned rampant crime, and in 1933, the Twenty-First Amendment to the constitution repealed the Eighteenth Amendment and turned control of alcohol back to the states).

1920s: Notable events include **women** gaining **voting rights** in 1920, and the **first winter Olympic Winter Games** in Chamonix, France in 1924. That same year, Native Americans were finally granted U.S. citizenship by the **Indian Citizenship Act** of 1924. The discovery of penicillin in 1928 ushered in the age of modern medicine.

In spite of prohibition, about two-dozen rollicking Park City saloons continued to illegally serve bootlegged booze during the "roaring twenties". Park City and its mining industry continued to prosper throughout the decade until the **stock market crashed** in 1929.

1930s: The **Great Depression** began in the United States but quickly lead to worldwide financial collapse. International trade plummeted fifty percent and there were big drops in the price of lead and silver, wounding Park City's economy.

President Franklin Roosevelt was elected in 1932 and initiated the **New Deal** to combat widespread unemployment and poverty. The Works Progress Administration (**WPA**) was a New Deal program that paid the unemployed to build needed **public works** such as schools, bridges and parks in almost every community in the country. The WPA built boarding houses in Park City and built the first ski trails for a winter carnival in 1936. (The WPA ended in 1943 when World War Two created a shortage of workers.)

In 1932, the **Great Lake Timber Company** briefly held the title of Park City's second largest employer, the mines being first. The timber company was called the "pole plant" because it provided utility poles to proliferating electric and telephone companies all over the western USA until it literally ran out of timber.

Alta Ski Area, in Little Cottonwood Canyon, a few miles south of Park City, opened its first ski lift in 1939, as war was breaking out in Europe.

1940s: The United States entered **World War Two** (1939-1945) after the Japanese bombed Pearl Harbor in 1941. President Roosevelt died in office, never seeing the war's end following the nuclear attack of **Hiroshima**, Japan by the United States in 1945.

The war helped bring about the recovery of the national economy, and in 1946, a T-bar ski lift was built out of some surviving tall trees, creating the **Snow Park Ski Area** on slopes that would ultimately become **Deer Valley Resort**. Lift tickets cost one dollar.

By the end of the decade, the price of silver and lead were spiraling downwards, and in the summer of 1949, more than a thousand miners were thrust out of work when the Park City **mines abruptly shut down**

1950s: Post war America was a time of economic growth and the rise of the middle class and suburbia, but not for Park City. Although some of the mines reopened, residents were moving away, and businesses were closing. Tourism further declined after authorities shut down the red-light district in 1955. While the rest of America was enjoying a baby boom, television, rock and roll, racial desegregation, polio immunization, and the rise of Las Vegas as the new **"sin city,"** Park City was considered to be a "ghost town."

1960s: The Viet Nam War, the Civil Rights movement, psychedelic pop culture and the assassination of President Kennedy marked this decade. To revive Park City's shattered economy, the last surviving mining company, **United Park City Mines,** procured a loan from the administration of **President John F. Kennedy** (1961-63) to open **Treasure Mountains Ski Area** in 1963. The longest gondola in the U.S.A. was installed, along with a double chair lift and a J-bar. Olympic ski celebrity **Stein Erikson** was hired as ski school director. Initially, lift tickets cost $3.50. The resort was renamed

Park City Ski Area in 1966. (When snowboarding became popular, the name was changed to **Park City Mountain Resort** in 1996.)

Park City's **mining history** is commemorated by many of the names of the resort's terrain. There are lifts and trails called Silver King, Silver Queen, Silver Star, Silver Skis, Silver Lode and Silver Hollow. Other mining associated names are: Prospector, Lost Prospector, Treasure Hollow, Glory Hole, Mother Lode, Bonanza, and Claim Jumper. Some monikers represent mining tools such as, Shaft, Hoist, Dynamite, Powder Keg, Nail Driver, and Widow Maker. The widow-maker was a drill that created enough silica dust to cause premature death from lung failure.

Ski slopes with names like Single Jack, Double Jack, Muckers, and Powder Monkey honor some of the **miners' jobs**. Before the pneumatic drill, miners blasted through rock by one man swinging a four-pound (1.8 kg) hammer against a drill bit, referred to as **"Single-Jacking." "Double Jacking"** describes two men doing this job, one swinging an eight-pound (3.6 kg) hammer and the other holding the drill bit against the rock. It took about fifty hammer strikes to be effective.

The **"Powder Monkey"** was the miner who handled the explosives. After a successful blast, a **"Mucker"** came along with a shovel to load the broken

rock into a mine car, as seen in this photo. As you might imagine, any "Tommy Knockers" haunting the resorts nowadays are much more likely to be "powder monkey" miners than powder skiers. Mining was and still is, one of the most dangerous jobs in the world.

Amongst the mining relics dotting Park City's ski slopes is the Silver King Boarding House, built in 1896. Featuring electricity and hot and cold running water, it was a marvel for its time. It used to provide meals to a thousand miners a day. In 1987, it was pushed up the mountain by bulldozers and renovated to become a slope side restaurant.

In 1968, **Park West Ski Area** opened just north of Park City Ski Area. After multiple changes of ownership and name, it became the **Canyons Village** at Park City Mountain Resort. Development is proliferating here.

1970s: Major events of this decade included the end of the war in Viet Nam, the beginning of the computer age, a gas shortage creating "oily" world politics, and the Watergate scandal and 1974 resignation of **President Richard M. Nixon.**

Back in Park City in 1974, a woman became a miner for the first time in the town's history, just as the mines were gasping their last breath. It took more than a hundred years and the **women's liberation** movement to squelch the superstition that females brought bad luck to mines.

1980s: This decade saw a nuclear disaster in Chernobyl, the collapse of Soviet communism, the birth of Microsoft Windows, and magnetic resonance imaging (MRI) became available to clinical medical practice.

Park City's ski resorts succeeded in bringing residents and tourists back to the town and in 1981, **Deer Valley Ski Area** was created with five lifts on Bald and Bald Eagle Mountains. Also in 1981, The Utah/US Film Festival moved from Salt Lake City to Park City, and later came under the direction of Robert Redford as the **Sundance Film Festival.**

Park City's recovery was also marked by the birth of its own radio station, KPCW, in 1980, and its own television station, TV45, in 1986.

1990s: Operation Desert Storm took place in Iraq and Kuwait, but the world was probably most changed by the creation of the **Internet** in 1991.

For Park City, the turn of the millennium was marked by residential expansion and the town's recognition as a winter sports mecca. Park City Mountain, Deer Valley, and The Canyons Resorts were frequently rated in the favorites lists of major winter sports publications.

2000s-Present: The successful **2002 Salt Lake City Olympic Winter Games**, staged six months after the 9/11 terrorist attacks, brought Park City international fame. The Deer Valley and Park City Mountain Resorts hosted most of the ski and snowboard events. The Utah Olympic Park in Kimball Junction provided venues for bobsled, luge, skeleton, and ski jumping. You can still watch athletes training at these facilities.

In 2008 *Forbes Traveler Magazine* named Park City one of the twenty **prettiest towns** in America.

Park City was designated a **Gold-Level Ride Center** by the International Mountain Bicycling Association in 2011. It was the first global biking destination to be so rated. Also in 2011, The *New York Times* featured an article ranking Park City as number nine of the 41 **top resort** places to go. In 2013 *Outside Magazine* selected Park City as the winner of the **Best Active Town** in America Award.

In 2015, after a historic corporate takeover, Vail Resorts built a gondola to connect Park City Mountain Resort with The Canyons Resort to create the **largest ski area** in the United States. Vail's presence in Park City augments the town's international stardom as Vail sells season passes globally, especially in the southern hemisphere where vacationers like to escape summer heat and spend a white Christmas in a ski town.

In 2015, *Fodor's Travel* identified 25 global "can't-miss" places to visit, rating the state of Utah as "The **Top Destination**" of the year. Also in 2015, Park City was designated the "**friendliest** place in America" by *Conde Nast Traveler Magazine*. Ever since, locals worry that this little town has attracted too many tourists and new residents, and not all of them are as friendly as was the town before it got added to every traveler's bucket list.

At the height of ski season in March 2020, Park City's resorts were abruptly closed due to recognition of the corona **virus pandemic**. Concerts, street fairs, and other Park City events were also cancelled in 2020, but as I revise this chapter in August 2020, I observe the town to be as busy as it tends to be any other summer if not busier. In the **age of COVID**, people are rediscovering the great outdoors and **walking** for recreation and exercise.

As you walk around Park City today, it may be difficult to visualize the tiny, primitive, polluted mining town that popped up here in the wilderness a century and a half ago, but the walks in this book will acquaint you with many of the landmarks that can connect you with the town and its colorful past history.

The Ecology of Park City

Walkers are likely to encounter geologic wonders and a variety of wildlife, vegetation, and weather phenomena as they walk around Park City.

ANIMALS

Birds are the animals most likely encountered on Park City walks, besides humans and dogs. Other abundant **critters** include chipmunks, squirrels, porcupines, marmots, foxes, rabbits, and little prairie dog-like critters called "potguts." Raccoons and skunks scavenge at night when the bats come out to eat the bugs.

Vegetarian **moose, elk** and **mule deer** reside in and around Park City. They often dine in people's yards and are too often encountered crossing roads.

Predatory coyotes, cougars (a.k.a. mountain lions), bobcats and black bears are occasionally observed in neighborhoods. Small children and pets are most at risk.

Muskrats and **trout** swimming in ponds and streams are common. You may also notice **beaver** dams along streams, but it's rare to see the nocturnal beaver.

Hunting is never legal in Park City and **fishing requires a license.**

Park City can be a nirvana for **birders.** Landscape variations and seasonal migrations provide a wide range of species. **Eagles, owls, osprey**, and **falcons** are seen on high perches, and a variety of hunting **hawks** challenge identification skills.

Sandhill crane couples return to their same nesting sites every spring.

Quail (mountain chickens) occasionally startle winter walkers by popping out of snowbanks and wild **turkeys** rule some local golf courses. Canada **geese** and **mallards** are regular residents, while many other waterfowl stop over during migration.

Birds most likely encountered include robins, sparrows, tree swallows, and mourning doves. The noisy, clever **magpie,** as in the photo on page 23, is one of Park City's most common residents. Regulars also include hummingbirds, chickadees, woodpeckers, killdeers, crows, ravens, grackles, flickers, kestrels, grosbeaks, red-winged blackbirds, and others too numerous to mention. **Bluebird houses** have been built along some trails to attract these beauties.

Critters you are **unlikely** to encounter in Park City include **biting insects** and **poisonous snakes** that prefer lower altitudes. Diamond back rattlesnakes have been observed at elevations just a little lower than Park City.

Traditional wildlife ranges may be altered by **climate change**, so there are no guarantees. Heavy rains can bring mosquitoes and it is likely that **encounters with wildlife will increase** as people build roads and homes deeper and deeper into the animals' habitat.

VEGETABLES

Park City's native vegetation varies widely, depending on the season, compass direction, and elevation. In this **high desert** environment, there's just enough precipitation in the form of mountain snow to support Park City's forests.

The **pine-oak belt** of trees predominates at Park City's lower elevations to the north and east. Starting around six thousand feet (1,829 m), Gambel oak and mountain mahogany tend to grow in thickets, providing food and shelter for deer. Rocky Mountain maple is also found at this elevation.

Closer to eight thousand feet (2,438 m), the **fir-aspen belt** prevails. Moose tend to hang out at the higher elevations where tall Douglas fir, subalpine fir, and Engelmann spruce dominate north-facing slopes and quaking aspens rule on the mountains' south sides.

A great variety of **wildflowers** can be found around Park City. Penstemon and paintbrushes (prairie fire) often provide a perfusion of blue and orange on north facing slopes.

Wild pink roses and multicolored columbine are common at higher altitudes. Wild geraniums and lupines border low-lying trails. Numerous sunflower species splash the landscape with yellow. Wild onions with lavender flowers are prolific in spring. Elderberry, chokecherry, snowberry and many other native and invasive plants grow in Park City's varied terrain.

Blooming seasons not only vary with elevation, but also from year to year, depending on temperature and precipitation levels. To catch the single week of summer that the prickly pears will be in bloom along west facing trails, I might have to walk there every week of June, or possibly miss this spectacular show. These same cacti bloom in an astounding array of colors a bit later on east facing trails.

The variety of wildflowers seen during different weeks of summer at different altitudes always amazes.

MINERALS

Park City is a living laboratory for **geology**, the study of Earth and its history by analysis of its rocks and land and water formations.

You can also play with the rocks and people sometimes build **cairns** (rock towers) as trails markers or, just for the fun of it.

The mountains and canyons we walk about in Park City were shaped by millions of years of geological processes including:

◊ the **deposition** of natural materials by ancient oceans,

◊ **uplift** of the mountains and sinking of the Salt Lake Valley along the **Wasatch Fault**,

◊ **transport** and **fracture** of rocks by **glaciers** and **rivers,** and

◊ continuous **erosion** by snow, rain and wind.

The discovery of precious metals in the rocks of Park City's rugged terrain gave birth to the town. Typically, it took **one ton** (907 kg) **of ore to produce one pound** (454 grams) **of silver**. From that same ton of ore, called **galena,** miners also recovered lead and zinc. However, hundreds of pounds (kilograms) of each ton of rock were useless (gangue). Such "**mine tailings**" can still be viewed as rock piles scattered around some local ski slopes.

The **bedrock** of this region consists of Jurassic quartzite, limestone, sandstone, siltstone, mudstone, and shale. Volcanic and glacial deposits add intrusive rocks to the top layers. Local terrain has been a commercial source of sandstone and you'll encounter some **quarries** along a few of the walks in this book.

Melting snow unearths **geologic history** every spring, and sometimes, human history. The observant walker might notice shells, marine fossils, ancient artifacts such as arrowheads, bits of galena, or perhaps, pieces of volcanic lava or meteorites. If walkers can shift their focal point from the magnificent macro-views most of these walks provide, a small treasure might be noticed, but should be left in place for the next observant eye.

WEATHER AND CLIMATE

Park City's climate can be dually classified. Its mountains retain a **temperate coniferous forest**, while the area's geographic location on the **Colorado Plateau** accords it a **high desert climate**.

Weather phenomena in Park City can include any of these conditions, at least some of which are likable:

Spectacular sunrises and sunsets occur almost daily. **Ultraviolet light** is more intense at altitude, and sunburn can occur even on cloudy days, especially if there's snow on the ground. **Sunscreen** is a must.

UV blocking sunglasses are also a must and should be worn on cloudy as well as bright days. The most protective sunglasses curve around the face and wrap around the temples to prevent UV exposure from the sides. They also have large enough lenses to reduce UV exposure from reflection off of the cheeks and forehead.

High heat in the late afternoon of long summer days is not a good time to

walk along rocky ridges or on black pavement, especially with dogs and children who are low to the ground. Mid-summer's hottest hours often occur between five and seven in the evening. However, even the rare very hot days usually start with deliciously cool mornings.

A **sundog** is a rainbow halo around the sun and/or bright spots on each side of the sun. Also known as a parhelion, this atmospheric phenomenon is created by the bending of light by ice crystals in high clouds. The appearance of a sundog may predict an impending storm.

Rapid temperature drops in the evening should be expected, even in mid-summer. Take an extra layer if you plan to walk as the sun disappears behind the mountains.

Lightning, sudden **downpours** and monster **hail** can occur any time of year but are most likely in hot weather. A wide brimmed, waterproof hat or thin plastic poncho can be a great asset on days with possibility of isolated thunderstorms. In the presence of lightening, get away from rocky ridges, open fields and lone trees. If you can't get indoors, you're safest crouching in a low place or a cluster of tall brush or small trees. Don't sit! You want minimal contact with the ground. Electrical storms occasionally occur in winter, shutting down ski lifts and delivering "thundersnow". Cells of precipitation can be so **isolated** that one chairlift might get six inches of snow while another chairlift gets a half-inch.

Virga is rain that evaporates before touching the ground, as observed from a distance. You may be walking in sunshine while watching cloudbursts around you.

Double rainbows often follow brief showers. Rainbows may occur whenever there are water droplets in the air and the sun is shining from a low point behind the observer, so even a fountain or sprinkler can create a rainbow. Look for rainbows in the eastern sky during early evening and the western sky in the morning. Double rainbows appear when light is reflected from within the raindrops as well as off of their surfaces. The second rainbow will show its colors as a mirror image of the first.

Inversions (of temperature) occur in winter when cold air gets trapped in low elevations. Park City can be ten or more degrees F (6-7 degrees C) cooler than Salt Lake City in the heat of summer, but just as many degrees warmer in winter. Ascending the mountains on inversion days can change the environment from cold, cloudy and smoggy, to warm, sunny and clear.

Artic Clippers are brief blasts of extremely cold air, that increase the risk for frostbite. For the most part, Utah winters are not bitter cold and a 32-degree F (0 degree C) day can feel warm when the sun is high.

Snow squalls are micro-storms of swirling snow that last a few minutes, usually in winter, but they can occur almost any time of year at higher elevations. **Blizzards** are actually infrequent in Utah, much to the chagrin of skiers. In recent years, Park City's snow has tended to fall in dribs and drabs as weather systems move rapidly through the mountains.

Avalanches may occur whenever there's snow in the mountains. Local news sources and websites provide avalanche risk reports daily in winter. You may also wake up to "dynamite reveille," on snowy mornings. That's the sound of explosions that ski patrollers set off in unstable snow to trigger avalanches before skiers can access steeper terrain. The Utah Avalanche Forecast Center and the U.S. Forest Service provide up-to-date information about avalanche risks at *utahavalanchecenter.org*.

Mudslides can occur with spring rains. **Rockslides** can occur with run-off, seismic vibration, or spontaneously.

Windstorms are most likely to occur in spring. Pockets of high winds can also be encountered along ridge tops and at the mouths of canyons. Since having the wind at your back when walking uphill is preferred, you may want to reverse the direction of the walks in this guide, depending on which way the wind blows. Prevailing winds come from the west, while some locales in Park City are prone to swirling winds.

Occasionally, an unexpected **microburst** of strong, **rogue wind** takes down trees or damages utilities. If walking on wooded trails on a windy day, be aware of the possibility of **falling trees**, especially in unhealthy looking woods. Throughout the western USA, aspens are in decline for a variety of reasons and many types of trees are succumbing to bark beetles.

Seismic tremors occur occasionally. Get down on all fours until the shaking stops. Get away from power lines, ski lifts and anything else that could fall should there be aftershocks. Be aware that even minor earthquakes can also trigger landslides and rockslides.

Fire is the number one threat to most communities in the western USA. While lightning and drought-stricken trees are primary risk factors, many fires are caused by thoughtless people who toss cigarettes, light firecrackers, fail to extinguish campfires, or go target shooting in fields of scorched earth on windy days.

Smoke from fires as far away as Siberia can sometimes be felt locally. In recent years, Park City's brilliantly blue skies have given way to almost chronically hazy conditions as the west falls deeper and deeper into drought and fire season gets longer and more intense.

On the day in September in 2020 that I updated this chapter, there were more than 600 fires burning in California, while additional smoke was being contributed by wildfires in Arizona, Idaho, Oregon, Washington and multiple places in Utah.

Rapid weather changes are entirely normal. Locals say: "if you don't like the weather, wait five minutes".

WARNING: Predictable weather and avalanche and fire conditions are reported by various local news and Internet sources daily. However, walkers must appreciate that the timing and localization of mountain weather is notoriously unpredictable.

Before You Go: Etiquette and Safety

Have a positive walking experience by observing the following rules and guidelines.

Don't tackle physical activity at high altitude that you are not accustomed to. If you are new to high altitude, especially if just arriving from sea level, be cautious. Even very fit persons can experience altitude sickness if they are genetically susceptible. Make sure you feel comfortable at Park City's elevation of 7,000 feet (2,134 m) before undertaking demanding exercise.

Headache, nausea, fatigue, insomnia, and shortness of breath are common symptoms of **altitude intolerance.** Drinking more water and going to a lower altitude will usually alleviate symptoms. Some altitude-sensitive persons will do best sleeping at a lower altitude and gradually increasing their daytime exposure to higher altitude. For others, dinner in Heber City at an elevation of about 5,600 feet (1,707 m), or Salt Lake City, at about 4,200 feet (1,280 m), may be just what the doctor orders.

Back in Park City, **smile at passersby**. Be patient and respectful. In neighborhoods unaccustomed to walkers, a friendly demeanor can allay suspicions.

Be prepared to **share roads** and **trails** with motorists, cyclists, dog walkers, skaters, skate boarders, equestrians, snow-shoers, snow-bikers, cross-country skiers, etc., and be warned: not all of them have read the rules. Cyclists and skiers can go very fast without making a sound, or wind might blow warnings out  of earshot. Some are inexperienced and can't stop, even though the walker has the right of way. When on busy paths or trails, use your ears for safety instead of music or conversation. Warn others when passing.

When **on roads**, walk towards oncoming traffic **on the left** side of the road. **On paved trails** pedestrians usually **walk on the right side**. Sometimes it's safest to get off of the path when cyclists or skiers coming from opposite directions have to pass each other.

When on busy trails or roadsides with narrow shoulders, **walk single file**. Also, consider that walking in large groups may be unsettling to neighborhoods or wildlife. A youth group leader might want to divide walkers into pairs and trios.

When allowing cyclists to pass on narrow single-track on hills, try to **step to the higher side of the trail** to reduce the risk of getting knocked downhill.

Road crossings are minimal for most of the walks in this guide. Use **crosswalks** and pedestrian controlled pushbuttons when available. Realize there are many tourists in Park City who may not be familiar with the roads, roundabouts, winter conditions, their rental vehicle, or driving on the right side of the road.

Even at crosswalks on quiet streets, walkers need to exercise caution. Try to **make eye contact** with drivers before entering a crosswalk to be sure they're

not distracted. If not on their phones, drivers might be gawking at the scenery or at spandex-clad cyclists; or gawking while on their phones.

Be visible. A driver, unaware they have early stage cataracts, may not be able to distinguish between the side of the road and a walker in gray pants and a green shirt. If you walk at dawn or dusk to watch the sun rise or set, like these darkly clad people, wear **reflective tape** in front and back. A blinking light on the black dog's collar also helps.

Respect fences, barricades and **"No Trespassing"** signs. All of the land around Park City is private property. Ownership and accessibility can change. If you mistakenly wind up on private land where a displeased owner confronts you, respectfully apologize and ask for instructions back to a public trail.

Respect the land. Forging a path up a steep slope as a shortcut to walking switchbacks may be quicker for you, but it causes **erosion**. When off-road, **stay on trails.**

Stay off muddy trails. In spring or after heavy rainfall, muddy trails can instantly become rutty. Bike tracks or footprints in mud can ruin a trail for the entire season and lead to erosion. If you encounter a muddy trail, turn around and find another place to walk.

Equestrians are occasionally encountered around Park City and all other trail users are obliged to yield to them. Horses spook easily. Do your best not to startle them. Take instructions from riders regarding passing.

No animal likes being snuck up on. Make some noise from a distance if you see a wild animal before she sees you, especially in spring when she might be protecting her babies, or in mating season in the fall.

Do not approach or **feed wild animals.** Wild animals that are not afraid of humans may be sick or rabid. Be extra alert at dawn and dusk when animals are more active. Walking in small groups is a good idea at these times, as is keeping your ears open to hear animal noise. Keep small kids and dogs close to the adults.

Never approach a carcass. A predator may be guarding its kill.

There may be signs at trailheads that advise specific behaviors for the possibility of encountering a potentially **dangerous wild animal.** Read and **heed these signs.**

Do not drink water from natural sources. Streams may contain high levels of heavy metals, the giardia parasite or other contaminants. There are streams along some of the walks in this book, but I prefer that my dogs don't drink this water and I always carry water for them.

Please share nature's gifts. Leave flowers unpicked and the pretty rock unturned for the next observer to enjoy. It's always sad to see a wilted bouquet of wildflowers thrown to the ground at the end of someone's walk. Even if you plunge them into your water bottle, wildflowers are fragile and will not survive much longer than the ride home.

Leave nothing behind. There are recycle containers, dog waste stations, and/or other waste receptacles at some trailheads and at most community facilities. If there isn't, take trash with you and dispose of it properly.

Winter walkers will be delighted to know that snow gets packed down on many miles of local trails. Find information about winter trail grooming and conditions at *mountaintrails.org* or *https://www.parkcity.org/departments/trails-open-space/winter-trails.*

On roads and sidewalks, winter walking conditions can be very variable with areas of dry pavement interspersed with **"black ice"** in shady spots. Black ice occurs when ice contains so little water that it doesn't glisten, and you can't see it. **Appropriate footwear** is critical to your safety, but even if you are very sure-footed and your shoes have excellent tread, you're no match for a skidding automobile on an icy hill. Be especially wary of icy conditions when the sun drops behind the mountains on warm winter afternoons.

High snowbanks that prohibit motorists exiting driveways or turning a corner from seeing pedestrians is another risk.

Mining relics dot Park City's landscapes and include old buildings, aerial tram towers, and mineshafts. Loose rocks traveling with spring run-off can expose mineshafts buried under rotted timbers. While effort has been made to reduce danger, walkers still need to **exercise caution** around such structures, some of which have collapsed in recent years.

Along with the rest of the Rocky Mountain region, Park City's native aspen and cottonwood trees are suffering blight. **Avoid walking in wooded areas on very windy days.** Occasionally, a rogue wind will knock down whole swarths of old trees. Sometimes, when deep in aspen glades, you don't feel the wind; but creaking and cracking sounds warn of tree distress.

Park City has traditionally been a very safe place to walk, if you discount slipping on ice while wearing inappropriate shoes. However, as a sometimes-lone walker, I am compelled to advise others: avoid **walking alone** in remote areas that you are not familiar with. If you walk alone, inform someone of where you are going and when you expect to be back, or leave behind information about your activity. Always carry with you the name and number of who to contact in case of emergency.

Pepper spray as a means of self-defense, requires a downwind position and relatively close proximity to a dangerous being. Still, it is recommended for walkers in bear territory. Alternatively, a **police whistle** might be helpful in some situations.

Personally, my only real **safety concern** for any of the walks in this book is **speeding cyclists** who do not give timely warnings. My concern about this issue has recently been increased by city hall's decision to allow electric bikes on non-motorized trails. Electric bikes should be applauded for boosting interest in cycling and allowing people with limited fitness to enjoy Park City's hilly terrain; but some such cyclists may not have the judgement or skill to navigate crowded narrow paths, necessitating increased caution on the part of walkers.

Staying alert and **attuned to the environment** and **anticipating the foibles of others is the best form of self-defense.**

Finally, your safety is always dependent on being **prepared for weather changes.** The chapter on Park City Ecology provides information about local weather phenomena.

WALKING WITH DOGS

Make sure your dog is healthy, fit, mature and obedient enough to be **safe** on the routes you choose.

All walking dogs are required to be on **leashes** in all public places including trails, with the exception of designated off-leash trails and dog-parks. Park City used to be such a dog-friendly place that it was affectionately called "Bark City". Unfortunately, irresponsible dog owners have ruined dog freedom for everyone. There are **leash police** in Park City who will ticket and fine owners of free-running dogs. If dogs are not going to be altogether banned from trail use, dog walkers should always take full responsibility for their pets' behavior and waste, even on dirt and snow-covered trails. Some trailheads provide poop-scooping bags (**mutt-mitts**), but please bring your own in case these aren't available.

It's recommended that if you walk an unfriendly dog that you put a yellow bandana or ribbon on the leash or collar. This **"yellow dog project"** is helpful to the nervous dog as well as to children or dog lovers who might otherwise approach the pooch who would be better off left alone.

Of all the walks in this book, I know of only a few short sections of trail that **disallow dogs** on leashes, and that's in some of the residential areas of the Deer Valley Duck Ponds, Walk #6. A few other walks herein are described as not ideal for dogs.

There are **off-leash dog-parks** available at Walk #22 Quinn's Junction, Walk #23 Willow Creek Park Loops, and Walk #29 Trailside Park. **Off-leash trails** are available at Trailside Park and on the Run-A-Muk Trails bordering the southeast side of Olympic Parkway. As of 2016, some Round Valley trails and the library field in town were opened to off leash dogs under voice control, on a trial basis.

It is **legal** for a shepherd, rancher or ranger **to kill a dog** that is harassing sheep, cattle, other livestock, or wildlife. Shepherds occasionally move flocks through Park City terrain. Goats have sometimes been employed for summer weed control. What dog wouldn't love to chase a goat? They're so much slower than deer and squirrels. Please protect yourself, pets, and others by leashing the dog.

Only certified service dogs are **allowed on** Park City's **buses**.*

WALKING COMBOS OR NOT?

Listening to music or books on tape or talking on the phone might be okay if you are familiar with your walking route, there's no traffic, you remain attentive to your surrounds, and you **leave one ear open**. Then again, a really exciting story or a heated conversation could compromise your awareness. Conversing or distracted walkers who can't hear warnings from others are at risk.

Reading or texting while walking is never a good idea, although a local college has designated a campus lane for that dual purpose. If you **must text** along the way, stop walking and **step out of the way.**

Whistling, singing, or playing the harmonica, castanets or tambourine might be okay if you are **not disturbing neighbors** or **wildlife** and you can **still hear** cars, bike bells, and voices.

Walkers can bird watch, people watch, business watch, construction watch, and/or neighborhood watch. **Watching** can be more absorbing than walking.

Entrepreneurs can be their own walking billboards. Town and mall walkers can **shop** along the way. **Mall walking** may facilitate sticking to a walking program in a controlled climate. Some urban walkers feel safer in malls with their long corridors of smooth surfaces.

Walking can provide sustenance to photographers, artists, writers, poets, composers, and other creative spirits. There is emerging evidence that **workers are more creative** and **productive** when walking is incorporated into their work schedules. Some organizations have started to hold walking meetings. My training as a physician taught me that learning is greatly enhanced when lessons are transferred from classrooms to walking around where the patients are.

Meditating, praying or engaging in **mental exercise** could be distractions or enhancements of the walking experience, depending on how you do it.

Going for a walk can be an emergency **anger management** tool for those moments in life when one contemplates worse behavior. However, if someone is too upset to pay attention to what they are doing, they shouldn't be out walking around.

The walker who seeks additional conditioning can add **stretching** and **rotation exercises** of the neck, torso, shoulders, arms, and hands. Breathing or facial exercises can also be incorporated. Pockets can accommodate stretch bands or squeeze putty to work the upper extremities, though serious walkers are adamant about the importance of the arms being able to swing freely and would not carry anything by hand, especially not weights.

The use of **walking poles** or **snowshoes** can add terrain and seasons to one's routine, as well as augment the development of stamina, strength and aerobic capacity; but there are other resources for that. This book is about basic walking.

Can you chew gum and walk at the same time? Although fatal asphyxiation due to **aspiration of candy** or **chewing gum** while walking is not as rare as it should be, there is some research that suggests chewing gum while walking can increase heart rate, and for older men, can increase walking speed and distance.

Keep in mind that **distracted walking is more dangerous than distracted driving.** In collisions, pedestrians are almost always the losers.

Using This Guidebook

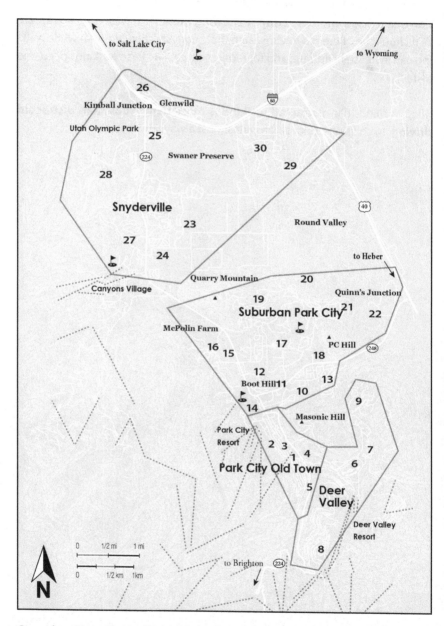

to Salt Lake City

to Wyoming

26

Kimball Junction   Glenwild

80

Utah Olympic Park

25

224   Swaner Preserve   30

28   29

Snyderville   40

23   Round Valley

27

24   to Heber

Canyons Village

Quarry Mountain   20

19   Quinn's Junction

Suburban Park City 21 22

McPolin Farm

16   17   PC Hill   248

15   18

12

Boot Hill 11

10   13

14

Masonic Hill   9

Park City
Resort   2 3   7

1 4   6

Park City Old Town

5 Deer
   Valley

Deer Valley
Resort

0   1/2 mi   1 mi

0   1/2 km   1km

N

to Brighton   224   8

Overview Map: The walks in this book are divided into four regions. This map shows the regions and the approximate location of each walk.

Map Legend

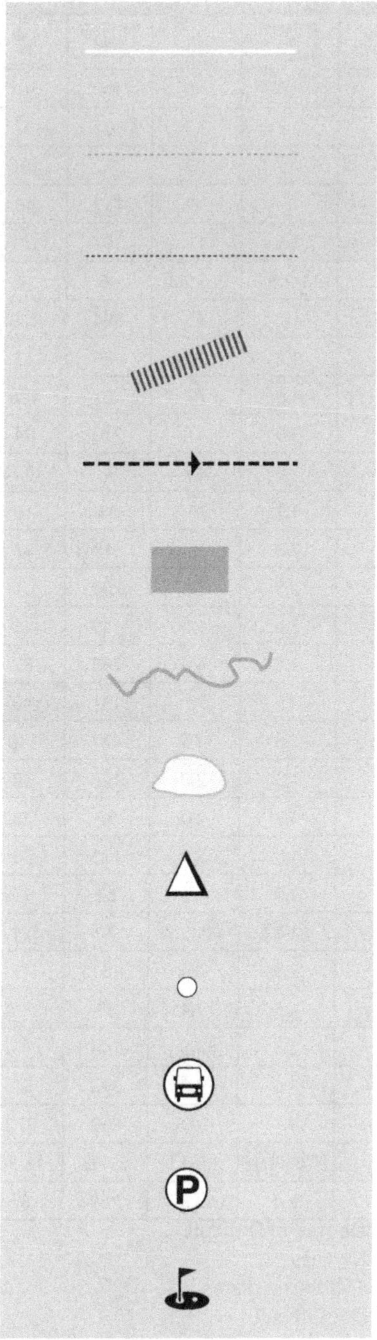

Paved Roads

Trails

Ski Lifts

Stairs

Route Direction

Preserved Open Space

Streams / Rivers

Ponds / Lakes

Mountain Tops / Hill Tops

Bus Stops

Transit Centers

Parking

Golf Courses

THE WALKS BY REGION* WITH DISTANCE, ELEVATION GAIN, AND DEGREE OF DIFFICULTY**

WALK	PAGE #	DEGREE OF DIFFICULTY**	DISTANCE IN MILES	DISTANCE IN KILO-METERS	ELEVATION GAIN IN FEET	ELEVATION GAIN IN METERS
1. City Park–Main Street	44	I	3.0	4.8	300	91
2. Old Town Via Park City Resort	48	D	2.2	3.5	302	92
3. Empire Ave–Park Ave	52	D	2.9	4.7	352	107
4. Masonic Hill–Deer Valley	56	D	2	3.2	152	46
5. Ontario Ridge–Rossie Hill	59	D	2.5	4.0	397	121
6. Deer Valley Duck Ponds	62	E	1-1.5	1.6-2.4	46	14
7. Deer Valley–Deer Crest	64	I	1.7	2.7	394	120
8. Silver Lake Village	67	E	1.2	1.9	43	13
9. Lower and Upper Deer Valley	69	I	4.8	7.7	387	186
10. Tour of Tunnels and Rail Trail	72	E	3.0	4.8	210	64
11. Olympic Plaza–Kearns Blvd	75	E	2.9	4.7	98	30
12. Boot Hill--McLeod Creek	79	I	1.2	1.9	33	10
13. Chatham Hills–Prospector Sq	82	I	2.8	4.4	318	97
14. Thaynes Canyon	85	I	2.5	3.8	200	61
15. Farm Trail–McLeod Creek Tr	88	I	3.5	5.6	148	45
16. Aspen Springs	92	I	2.5	4.0	285	87
17. Park Meadows	95	I	4.9	7.9	131	40
18. PC Hill	98	D	2.8	4.5	427	130
19. The Cove–Quarry Mountain	101	I	1.3	2.0	125	38
20. La Dee Duh	104	I	1.3	2.0	92	28
21. Fairway Hills	107	E	1.8	2.9	125	38
22. Quinn's Junction	110	E	1.0	1.6	62	19
23. Willow Creek Park	112	E	0.3-1.8	0.5-2.9	70	21
24. Matt Knoop Pk–McLeod Crk	114	E	2.5	4.0	161	49
25. Swaner Preserve–Redstone	117	E	1.5	2.4	33	10
26. Over/Under Kimball Junction	119	E	2.8	4.5	148	45
27. The Canyons–Sun Peak	122	D	3.0	4.8	272	83
28. Bear Hollow–Olympic Park	125	D	6.7	10.8	892	272
29. Trailside Park	128	E	0.65-1.1	1.0-1.8	59-98	18-30
30. Mountain Ranch Estates	130	I	2.4	3.8	269	82

*Regions:
Old Town   #s 1-5
Deer Valley   #s 6-9
Suburban Park City   #s 10-22
Snyderville Basin   #s 23-30

**Degree of Difficult
E = Easy
I = Intermediate
D = Difficult

Like the rating system for ski trails, **degree of difficulty is relative** only to the mountain you're on. The difficulty of these walks has been assessed with respect to distance, elevation gain, trail surface, and how each walk compares to the other included walks.

THE WALKS BY DISTANCE STARTING WITH THE SHORTEST					
Walk Name	Walk #	Page #	Difficulty*	Distance In Miles	Distance In Kilometers
Willow Creek Park	23	112	E	.33-1.83	.5-2.9
Trailside Park	29	128	E	.65-1.12	1.0-1.8
Quinn's Junction	22	110	E	1	1.6
Deer Valley Duck Ponds	6	62	E	1-1.5	1.6-2.4
Boot Hill–McLeod Creek	12	79	I	1.15	1.9
Silver Lake Village	8	67	E	1.16	1.9
The Cove–Quarry Mountain	19	101	I	1.3	2.0
La Dee Duh	20	104	I	1.3	2.0
Swaner Preserve–Redstone	25	117	E	1.48	2.4
Deer Valley–Deer Crest	7	64	I	1.7	2.7
Fairway Hills	21	107	E	1.8	2.9
Masonic Hill–Deer Valley	4	56	D	2	3.2
Old Town Via Park City Resort	2	48	I	2.3	3.7
Mountain Ranch Estates	30	130	I	2.38	3.8
Thaynes Canyon	14	85	I	2.4	3.8
Ontario Ridge–Rossie Hill	5	59	D	2.4	3.8
Aspen Springs	16	92	I	2.5	4.0
Matt Knoop Park–McLeod Crk	24	114	E	2.54	4.0
Chatham Hills–Prospector Sq	13	82	I	2.75	4.4
Over/Under Kimball Junction	26	119	E	2.8	4.5
PC Hill	18	98	D	2.82	4.5
Olympic Plaza–Kearns Blvd	11	75	E	2.85	4.7
City Park–Main Street	1	44	I	3	4.8
Tour of Tunnels and Rail Trail	10	72	E	3	4.8
The Canyons–Sun Peak	27	122	D	3	4.8
Empire Avenue–Park Avenue	3	52	D	3.38	5.2
Farm Trail–McLeod Creek Trail	15	88	I	3.45	5.6
Lower and Upper Deer Valley	9	69	I	4.8	7.7
Park Meadows	17	95	I	4.87	7.9
Bear Hollow–Olympic Park**	28	125	D	**6.75	**10.8

*Degree of Difficulty
    E=Easy
    I=Intermediate
    D=Difficult

** **Bus Service** can cut Route
#28 to about 3 miles (4.8 km)

The **easiest** walks tend to have level surfaces and gentle inclines. Pavement is usually smooth enough for wheelchairs or strollers. Unpaved trails are without big rocks and roots. Some trails are groomed in winter making them accessible to short legs and ordinary winter shoes. For **winter trail information** check *mountaintrails.org* or *https://www.parkcity.org/departments/trails-open-space/winter-trails*.

Walks of **intermediate** difficulty have inclines that are longer and/or steeper, but still manageable for moderately fit walkers.

For more **difficult routes**, walkers should be in good health and well-conditioned. These walks involve long or steep inclines, longer distances, higher altitudes, or rougher terrain.

THE WALKS IN ORDER OF ESTIMATED DEGREE OF DIFFICULTY			
EASY	**EASY TO INTERMEDIATE**	**INTERMEDIATE TO DIFFICULT**	**DIFFICULT**
23. Willow Creek Pk.	1. City Park-Main St.	7. DV*-Deer Crest	5. Ontario Ridge
22. Quinn's Junction.	14. Thaynes Canyon	13. Chatham Hills	2. Old Town
6. DV* Duck Ponds	30. Mt Ranch Estates	12. Boot Hill	18. PC Hill
8. Silver Lake	15. Farm-McLeod Cr.	17. Park Meadows	3. Empire-Park
29. Trailside Park	20. Lah Dee Duh	16. Aspen Springs	27. The Canyons
25 Swaner-Redstn	19. Cove-Quarry Mt.	9. Low & Up DV*	28. Olympic Park
21. Fairway Hills		4. Masonic Hill	
11. Oly Plaza-Kearns			
24. Matt Knoop Park			
26. Kimball Junction			
10. Tour of Tunnels	* DV = Deer Valley		

Time allotments for these walks are not specified. For the average leisure walker, 20-25 minutes per mile (1.6 km) is typical. Some people will need less than half or twice that amount of time.

Walkers may find historic features, or shopping and dining along some of these walks. Check this table of **popular walk features** to find walks that are friendly to kids, dogs, or in snowy conditions. Routes not designated off-road are on paved surfaces.

Popular Walk Features	Dining	Dogs+	Historic	Kids^	Off-Road	Shopping	Wheels	Winter*
1. City Park-Main Street								
2. Old Town Via PC Resort								
3. Empire Ave-Park Ave					M			
4. Masonic Hill-Deer Valley								
5. Ontario Ridge-Rossi Hill								
6. Deer Valley Duck Ponds								
7. Deer Valley-Deer Crest					M			
8. Silver Lake Village								
9. Lower & Upper DV					M			
10. Tour of Tunnels & Rail Trl								
11. Olympic Plaza-Kearns Blvd					M			
12. Boot Hill-McLeod Crk Trl								
13. Chatham Hills-Prospector					M		S	
14. Thaynes Canyon					M		S	
15. Farm Trl-McLeod Crk Trl								
16. Aspen Springs							S	
17. Park Meadows								
18. PC Hill								
19. The Cove-Quarry Mt								
20. La Dee Duh								
21. Fairway Hills								
22. Quinn's Junction		P						
23. Willow Creek Park		P			M			
24. Matt Knoop-McLeod Crk					M			
25. Swaner-Redstone								
26. Over/Under Kimball Jncn					M		S	
27. The Canyons-Sun Peak							S	
28. Bear Hollow-Olympic Pk							S	
29. Trailside Park		P						
30. Mountain Ranch Estates							S	

+ = dog preferred   P = dog park/trail
^ kids = playgrounds, courts   M = minimal off-road
S = smooth but steep for strollers or wheelchairs
* = conditions permitting, snow may be packed down or cleared

ABOUT THE INFORMATION IN THIS BOOK

Many of these walks are accessible by Park City's **free bus transportation**. Bus schedules and **routes vary seasonally** and can be altered by special events. Find information at *parkcity.org/departments/transit-bus/routes-schedules*, or at *go.parkcity.org/InfoPoint/*, or on signs at bus stops, and on brochures inside the buses. Buses are equipped to carry wheelchairs and a limited number of bicycles. Only certified service animals are allowed on buses. In directions, bus stop names are *italicized*.

Parking information is given for all walks. However, Park City is rapidly becoming **"Do Not Park City."** Some free parking space convenient to trails is being consumed by development, while paid parking is both limited and expensive. Parking in an unauthorized place often results in extremely costly towing. Some of the walks in this book rely on free summer parking at the ski resorts, but resort parking lots are slated for development, and paid parking will likely be all that's left in the future. Having someone drop you off or using a driver service may be the best way to access some walking routes.

Maps of the walks in this guide identify bus stops, parking areas, and other landmarks where applicable. Landmarks, parking areas, and bus stops and routes are all **subject to change**. Distances and elevations are approximate. They were computed using the smart phone app *mapmywalk.com*. Fractions are rounded off. If you track these same walks using any GPS app, readings may differ. **Trail names are bolded** to distinguish them from road names.

Directions are often given in terms of the **compass.** If you're unsure of the direction when the sun's position isn't obvious, remember that Park City's bigger mountains are to the west and south.

All of the walks in this book are configured as loops that bring you back to start. Please don't wander into off-road terrain without consulting appropriate resources to ensure that you don't become an illegal intruder, lost, or carried off by a rockslide.

If you are interested in accessing more mountainous terrain, my second book, *Park City Hiking Guide*, is sold by various Park City merchants and by major online booksellers. Also, the trail map produced annually by the nonprofit **Mountain Trails Foundation** is sold locally in

sporting goods stores. Sales of the map help support the trail system. At the website *mountaintrails.org,* find interactive maps and up-to-date information about trail conditions or closures due to mud, maintenance or events like races. Park City's **trail system is complex** and **difficult to navigate** without assistance.

Restrooms are available for most of these walks as described, and for most of these walks, privacy is available only in restrooms.

NOTICE:

Trails, paths, roads and landmarks noted for any of the **routes** in this book **are subject to change.** New construction, property ownership change, or natural phenomena may delete or reroute any of these walks. Maps on GPS satellite systems, as well as maps in this book, may lag behind changes in roads, and trails.

Bus stops, bus routes and parking areas have been undergoing reductions and other **changes** in recent years.

Street **signs** and trail markers aren't always present and occasionally **get twisted** around to point the wrong way.

Wildlife might create new **"fooler" trails** when nature provides them a new food source. Sometimes people create new trails that confuse these directions. Please don't do that.

Please respect barricades, signs, ropes, etc. indicating Private Property or No Trespassing.

#1 City Park – Main Street

DESCRIPTION: If you only take one of the 30 walks in this book, this should be it. You'll experience some of the best recreational and cultural delights that Park City has to offer. Expect to spend more time than the distance suggests if you're inclined to read menus, explore galleries and
boutiques, take pictures, and/or watch athletes fly around a skate park.

Distance: 3.0 miles (4.8 km)

Elevation Gain: 300 feet (91 m)

Peak Elevation: 7,188 feet (2,192 m)

Difficulty: INTERMEDIATE. Walk up a gentle incline for the first mile and then the free Main Street Trolley could be an option. Most people are too busy enjoying Main Street's amenities to be bothered by the 1 1/2 miles (2.4 km) it takes to experience it from end to end.

Surface: Paved surfaces except for occasional construction walkways.

Restrooms are available in City Park, south of the Park City Museum on the east side of Main Street, down a staircase, and in Miners Park on the west side of Main Street.

NOTABLE FEATURES:

◊ Park City's **City Park** at the north end of Old Town provides **playgrounds, sports** fields and courts, a five-tier **skate park**, an amphitheater and **picnic** facilities. It's also the relocation site of **Miners Hospital** where thousands of miners with injuries and "Miners' Con" (consumption of the lungs) were cared for in the old days.

◊ **Poison Creek Trail** is an artist-decorated paved path from City Park to Old Town. This delightful trail with its unfortunate name borders a stream that was previously polluted by the mining industry and outhouses along its banks.

◊ **Shoe Tree Park** on the east side of Poison Creek was built around a custom that started in the 1960s when some locals flung shoes into a tree. In 2011, disapproving residents persuaded Park City officials to remove enough footwear to fill 26 big garbage bags, but the trees were quickly redecorated with all kinds of footwear, even ski boots. It seems that Shoe Tree Park has become an ongoing conflict between residents who cherish this custom and less appreciative newcomers. Perhaps the shoes won't be there when your walk, but you can still enjoy a **picnic** park built around the trees.

◊ **Historic Main Street** offers a smorgasbord of restaurants, art galleries, exclusive boutiques, and souvenir shops. A calendar of gallery tours and special events is available on the website of the Chamber of Commerce at *visitparkcity.com.*

◊ The **Park City Museum**, 528 Main Street, (*parkcityhistory.org*), provides exhibits of the town and life in old Park City, including a mock-up of a mine and an interactive map that shows more than a thousand miles (1,609+ km) of mining tunnels beneath the resorts. Tour the territorial jail preserved in the museum basement to see the less romantic side of the Old West. Rotating traveling exhibits are featured in the Museum's Tozer Gallery. This museum was originally City Hall, built in 1885.

◊ The **Egyptian Theatre**, 328 Main Street, (*egyptiantheatercompany.org*), was built in 1926. Egyptian décor became a global fashion with the 1922 discovery of King Tut's 3,000+ year-old intact tomb. (King Tutankhamun ruled Egypt c.1332-1323 BC.)

◊ The **Wasatch Brew Pub**, 250 Main Street, was established in 1986, the first brewery in Utah and one of the first craft brewers in the country. The microbrewery movement started in the UK in the 1970s. Today there are about 3,000 independent craft brewers in the U.S.A.

◊ The **Imperial Hotel** at 221 Main Street was a miners' boarding house in the early 1900s.

◊ **Park City Live**, 427 Main Street, occupies the War Veterans Memorial Building, constructed in 1939 with federal funding. This building previously housed Boy Scouts, the American Legion, and a bowling alley. It now serves as a venue for top name entertainment.

◊ The **Union Pacific Railroad Depot**, (The Depot), 660 Main Street, functioned as a railroad station from 1886 until the mid 1970s. In 1986, the last train rolled out of Park City, after which this building was converted to a restaurant.

DIRECTIONS:

- From **bus stop 1520**, *Park Ave at 7-11,* walk around and behind the 7-11 store. Find a ball field. Take the path alongside the field and it bends left towards tennis courts.

- **Drivers** turn south off of Deer Valley Drive and park at the north end of City Park near the tennis courts.

- Start on the paved path that passes tennis courts to the left. Come to an intersection with another paved path.
- Turn right heading south on this path, the **Poison Creek Trail**. Pass sports fields and a skate park. At a fork showing Main Street to the right, bear left towards the **Lost Prospector Trail**.
- At a second fork with a basketball court to the right, bear left and come to another fork showing Deer Valley to the left.
- Bear right to arrive on Heber Avenue. Walk to the intersection with Main Street.
- Cross Heber Avenue to walk up the east side of Main Street, (or take the free trolley).
- At the top of Main, cross the street and walk downhill, re-crossing Heber Avenue and continuing onto Lower Main Street. Pass the Town Lift Plaza and come to an intersection with 9th Street.
- Turn left onto 9th. Follow it around a curve to intersect with Park Avenue.
- Turn right going north on Park Avenue for multiple **bus** stops. **Drivers** should continue to the next right corner, Sullivan Road (an extension of 12th Street).
- Turn right onto Sullivan. The sidewalk alternates from left to right around parking and brings you back to start.

ROUTE SUMMARY:

o   Start in the north end of City Park at the tennis courts.

o   Pass the courts and turn right onto the Poison Creek Trail.

o   Bear left at two forks showing Main Street to the right. At a third fork, bear right onto Heber Avenue. Head west towards Main Street.

o   Turn left onto the east side of Main Street.

o   At the top of Main, cross the street to descend on the west side.

o   Cross Heber Avenue to lower Main Street and continue to 9th Street.

o   Turn left onto 9th Street and follow to an intersection with Park Avenue.

o   Turn right onto Park Avenue to find a bus stop or come to Sullivan Road.

o   Drivers turn right onto Sullivan and follow it north to the tennis court parking.

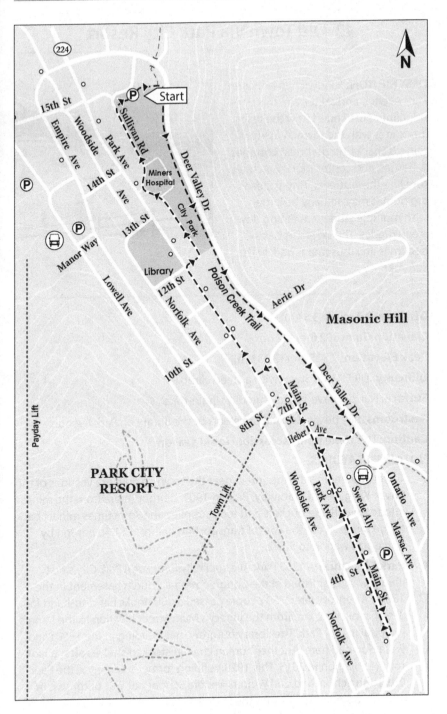

#1 City Park – Main Street

#2 Old Town Via Park City Resort

DESCRIPTION: Sandwiched between Park Avenue and ski terrain, this ridgeline route shows how the resort integrates with the town. A mixture of miner's shacks, gingerbread cottages, A-frames, and contemporary architecture line these streets. Tiny appearing homes may actually be large, with multiple stories cascading down steep grades. The ski resort base becomes an amusement park in the summer.

Distance: 2.2 miles (3.5 km)

Elevation Gain: 302 feet (92 m)

Peak Elevation: 7,325 feet (2,233 m)

Difficulty: DIFFICULT. Starts with a steep climb.

Surface: Narrow paved roads and dirt single-track.

Restrooms may be available at the resort or the library on Park Avenue.

Caution: This route is **not accessible in ski season.**

NOTABLE FEATURES:

◊ Towers ascending the mountain near the town chairlift are vestiges of the **Silver King Aerial Tramway**. Built in 1901, it brought ore from the mines into town in flying buckets and took supplies and sometimes miners back to the mines. It cut the cost of transporting ore from $1.50 per ton by horse and wagon to $0.22.

◊ **Park City Library**, 1255 Park Ave. (*parkcitylibrary.org*) Park City's first library was established in the Congregational Church basement in the 1880s. A century later, 750 people passed 5,000 books hand-to-hand for 3/4 of a mile (1.2 km) from the library's Main Street location to the Miners Hospital in City Park. The library outgrew that building in the 1990s and was relocated here. Another human chain restocked shelves after a high-tech renovation in 2015. This 1928 building formerly served as the Park City High School and Carl Winters Middle School but was outgrown in 1981. In addition to housing the library, the school auditorium serves as a community theater.

◊ **Chateau Après Lodge**, 1299 Norfolk Avenue, was one of the first skier hotels built in conjunction with the opening of Park City Ski Area in the 1960s.

◊ **Park City Resort** (*parkcitymountain.com*) offers lodging, dining and shopping. Additional seasonal amenities include an alpine slide, alpine coaster, zip line, scenic lift rides, lift assisted hiking and cycling, horseback riding, miniature golf, a climbing wall, and other amusement park activities. Business are open primarily during ski season and variably in summer.

DIRECTIONS:

- **Drive** to Park City Resort or exit at **bus stop 1000**, *PC Mountain*. At the southwest corner of the parking area, find the intersection of Lowell Avenue and Manor Way.

- Walk south up Lowell until it becomes a dirt path, just right of a residential driveway as the road bends left. Continue up this steep but short dirt path. Ignore some turnoffs to the right and left. Find a fork at the crest.

- Bear right at the fork (but not extreme right) and you'll be on a tree-lined trail, looking down on the town. The trail ends on Norfolk Avenue. Continue south on Norfolk and after it bends right, arrive at an intersection with King Road.

- Turn left onto King and proceed to the next intersection, Woodside Avenue.

- Turn left onto Woodside and follow it around a right bend where it intersects with Park Avenue. After a rock wall, notice a dirt/gravel footpath to the left.

- Turn left onto the footpath. It takes you past the west end of the ski bridge under the chairlift, crosses a ski trail, and then descends to end at the intersection of Crescent Tram and Woodside Avenue.

- Turn left onto Crescent Tram, (8th Street), and proceed to the next intersection with Norfolk Avenue.

- Turn right onto Norfolk and proceed north, passing the back of the Park City Library. At the corner of 13th Street, (Calhoun Street), look for a staircase to your left.

- Climb the staircase to Empire Avenue and turn right to return to **parking** or the **bus** at the resort base.

ROUTE SUMMARY:

o   Start at the intersection of Lowell Avenue and Manor Way.

o   Proceed south on Lowell to the dirt trail, just before Lowell bends left. Ascend the trail onto a dirt path.

o   Bear right where the path forks and follow this trail until it ends on Upper Norfolk Avenue. Proceed to King Road.

o   Turn left onto King and proceed to Woodside Avenue.

o   Turn left onto Woodside and continue past a right bend and rock wall to find a footpath on the left.

o   Take the footpath under the chairlift and descend to an intersection with Crescent Tram (8th Street).

o   Turn left onto Crescent Tram and proceed to Norfolk Avenue.

o   Turn right onto Norfolk and pass the library.

o   Take the staircase on your left at the intersection of Norfolk and 13th Street.

o   At the top of the stairs, turn right onto Empire to return to start.

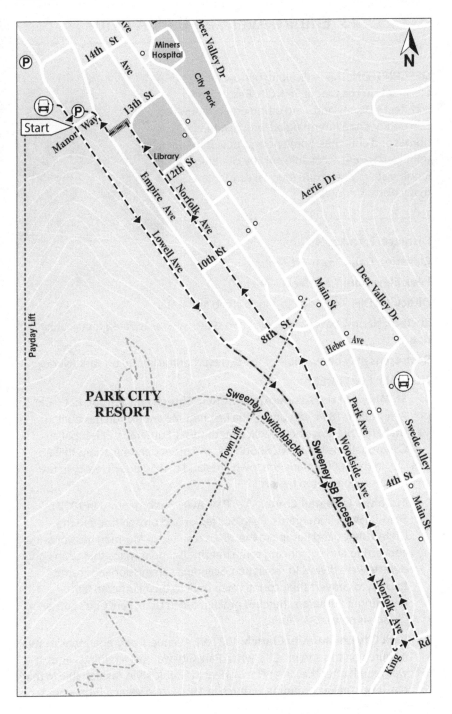

#2 Old Town Via Park City Resort

#3 Empire Avenue – Park Avenue

DESCRIPTION: This walk along narrow residential streets at the foot of Park City Resort is an architect's Disneyland. Find ultramodern mountain engineering intermingled with historic homes and churches. Some houses built into uphill terrain are accessible only by climbing lengthy stairs. The return loop takes you past many historic addresses.

Distance: 2.9 miles (4.7 km)

Elevation Gain: 352 ft. (107 m)

Peak Elevation: 7,349 feet (2,240 m)

Difficulty: DIFFICULT due to a long climb at the start.

Surface: Narrow paved roads plus two staircases, (of serrated metal, unkind to dog feet).

Restrooms may be available at the ski resort or the library on Park Avenue.

NOTABLE FEATURES:

◊ **St. Mary's of the Assumption Catholic Church** and **School**, 121 Park Ave, built in 1884, was one of the first non-Mormon churches built in Utah. The presence of Catholics, Methodists, Lutherans, Episcopalians, Congregationalists, Jews, Buddhists, and other denominations in Park City in the 1800s, made the town an island of religious diversity in the Mormon dominated region.

◊ **St. John's Lutheran Church**, 323 Park Ave., was organized in 1902 by Scandinavian immigrants. Religious fervor and proselytizing in the United States and Europe in the 1800s resulted in Mormon missionaries converting and convincing some freezing Scandinavians that Utah's deserts were divine. In retaliation, Scandinavian missionaries came to Utah to convert their countrymen back to their Lutheran faith. Resultingly, Lutheran churches proliferated in Utah. Park City's Lutheran Church is now in its suburbs.

◊ **Park City Community Church**, 402 Park Avenue. Congregationalists built a church on this site in 1883, when Park City was just a mining camp. It was rebuilt after the Great Fire of 1898 in Gothic style, fashionable in that era. It became a community church in 1919 when several Protestant sects united. The building passed into private hands after a new church was built in Snyderville in the 1990s.

◊ **The Blue Church**, 427 Park Avenue, was constructed in 1897 as a Mormon meetinghouse, was lost in the Great Fire of 1898, and rebuilt in 1899. The Mormon congregation moved to bigger quarters in 1962. After housing a dance studio and then an art museum, the blue church was converted to condominiums.

◊ **St. Luke's Episcopalian Church**, 523 Park Ave., also Gothic in style, was originally located two blocks south. It was rebuilt here in 1901 after the Great Fire and modernized in 1978.

◊ **Washington School House**, 543 Park Ave, was built in 1889, as one of Park City's first schools. From 1936 through the 1950s it was a VFW (Veterans of Foreign Wars) social hall. It opened as the Washington School Inn in 1985. It's now a luxury hotel.

◊ **High West Distillery**, 703 Park Ave, is also a restaurant at the bottom of the Quittin' Time ski run. In the early 1900s, this building served as a livery stable for horses that pulled heavy carts of ore. With the arrival of the automobile it became a gas station from 1915 to 1942. It served as a residence before becoming the distillery of award-winning spirits.

◊ As in Walk #2, a segment of **Woodside Avenue** is included in this route as it's one of the town's few connector streets. Woodside is steeped both in history and terrain. Some of Park City's wealthiest citizens built homes here in the 1880s. **Historic** addresses are identified by ribbons as seen in this photo.

◊ **Park City Resort** at the start and end of your walk offers dining and entertainment as noted in Walk #2.

DIRECTIONS:

- **Drive** to Park City Resort or exit at **bus stop 1000**, *PC Mountain*. At the southeast corner of the parking, find the intersection of Manor Way and Empire Avenue.
- Turn right onto Empire Avenue. Proceed until it intersects with Crescent Tram, south of 10th Street on the left.
- Turn left onto Crescent Tram, (8th Street), a winding road that was once a narrow-gauge railroad for transporting ore. Proceed to the intersection with Norfolk Avenue.

- Turn right onto Norfolk. Walk toward a house at the end of the street. To the right of the house, find a paved trail that becomes dirt and gravel on the way to Woodside Avenue.
- Continue south on Woodside. Pass several long down staircases on the left. Towards the end of the street, notice a crosswalk and fire hydrant on the right, at the foot of a staircase that goes up and down. This route goes up. (If you're not game to ascend 117 steps, you can descend the steps here and come out on Park Avenue. Turn left onto Park and skip to the directions four steps below.) If you ascend the steps, turn left onto Upper Norfolk Avenue at the top.
- Proceed a short distance on Upper Norfolk to a right-hand turn, Sampson Avenue, which goes off diagonally (and can be confused with private driveways.)
- Turn right onto Sampson and ascend for a short distance; then Sampson rolls downhill and around a switchback. Come to a W-intersection with King Road and Ridge Avenue.
- Take the far left turn onto Ridge and follow it downhill as it bends into Daly Avenue.
- Turn left onto Daly Avenue which ends at an X-intersection with Main Street to the right and Park Avenue to the left.
- Bear left onto Park Avenue and proceed to 13th Street.
- Turn left onto 13th Street and walk uphill to a staircase. Climb the stairs and turn right at the top to get to **parking** and the **bus** at Park City Resort.

ROUTE SUMMARY:

o   Start at the intersection of Empire Avenue and Manor Way.
o   Proceed onto Empire Avenue going south.
o   Turn left onto Crescent Tram.
o   Turn right onto Norfolk Avenue. Proceed to the end.
o   Look to the right for a sidewalk to Woodside Avenue. Proceed on Woodside to an up-staircase next to a fire hydrant on your right.
o   Turn left onto Upper Norfolk at the top of the stairs.
o   Turn right onto Sampson Avenue and proceed to a W-intersection.
o   Take the extreme left turn onto Ridge Avenue.
o   Turn left onto Daly Avenue and proceed to the X-intersection.
o   Bear left onto Park Avenue at the X.
o   Turn left onto 13th Street heading west.
o   Ascend a staircase and turn right to return to start.

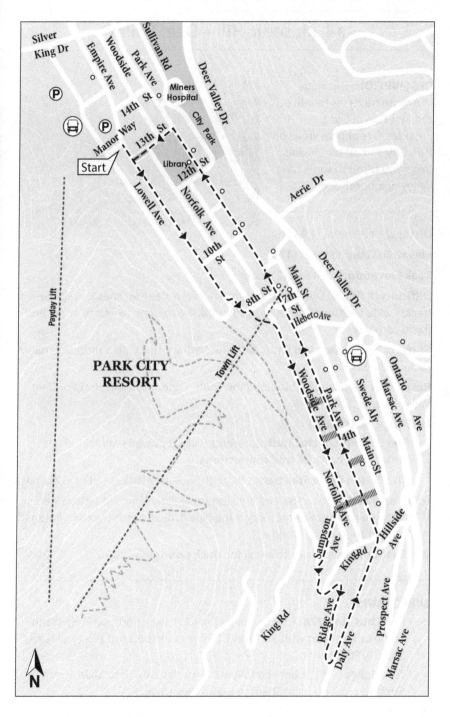

#3 Empire Avenue – Park Avenue

#4 Masonic Hill – Deer Valley

DESCRIPTION: This ridge-line route traverses terrain on the east side of Old Town. It provides exceptional views of Park City and ski terrain and takes you through some Deer Valley neighborhoods.

Distance: 1.86 miles (2.93 km)

Elevation Gain: 155 feet (47 m)

Peak Elevation: 7,204 feet (2196 m)

Difficulty: INTERMEDIATE due to some short but steep inclines and single-track. Tackle the steep part at the beginning if you come by bus or at the end if you come by car.

Surface: Paved roads and paths and a single-track trail with a short but mildly rocky incline.

Restrooms are not available along this route. Detour to Main Street or Deer Valley Plaza.

NOTABLE FEATURES:

◊　The **Lost Prospector Trail** represents Park City's well-maintained trail system and provides **trail connections**.

◊　The **Poison Creek Trail** passes through Shoe Tree Park as noted in Walk #1.

◊　**Masonic Hill** was so named because some early Mormon settlers were also freemasons. Freemasonry is the oldest, most participated-in fraternal organization in the world.

◊　**Detour** to Deer Valley to enjoy the **duck ponds** of Walk #6.

DIRECTIONS:

- From **bus stop 778**, *Park Avenue at Town Lift*, walk north on Park Avenue to the intersection with 9th Street. (There could be a bus stop on Main Street & 9th Street)

- Turn right on 9th Street and follow it as circles around to Main Street. Continue east on Main Street to Deer Valley Drive.

- Turn left and walk north along Deer Valley Drive until you see an uphill road across the street. Carefully cross Deer Valley Drive and proceed onto

Aerie Drive.

- **Drivers** turn east off of Deer Valley Drive onto Aerie Drive and find limited parking immediately to the right. If unavailable, park in Old Town and walk back.

- The **Lost Prospector Trail** is on both sides of Aerie Drive. Ascend to the trail on the south (right) side. Proceed up a short, steep single-track until you come to a double-track.

- Turn left onto the double-track.

- Quickly turn right at the next intersecting single-track. Pass below a water tank and cross a dirt road, after which the trail bends right and ends on Mellow Mountain Road.

- Continue downhill on the curves of Mellow Mountain to Sunnyside Drive.

- Turn right onto Sunnyside and proceed downhill to Deer Valley Drive.

- Cross Deer Valley Drive, turn right and follow the sidewalk downhill to a roundabout.

- Carefully cross at crosswalks three times in the roundabout. Then bear right and quickly turn left to go north on the **Poison Creek Trail**. Look for a fire hydrant next to a staircase on the left, after passing Shoe Tree Park.

- Ascend the stairs onto a plaza with a ramp to Main Street, which bends right.

- **Bus** riders should turn left onto Main Street and follow it to 9th Street, then back to Park Avenue where there are several bus stops.

- **Drivers** should turn right, cross Main Street and proceed to its northeast corner. Then turn left onto Deer Valley Drive and cautiously cross it to ascend Aerie Drive to your car.

ROUTE SUMMARY:

o   Start on the Lost Prospector Trail on the south side of Aerie Drive.

o   Turn right onto this single-track and proceed to an intersection with a double-track.

o   Turn left and quickly turn right, back onto single-track. Follow it to Mellow Mountain Road.

o   Proceed downhill on Mellow Mountain to Sunnyside Drive.

o   Turn right onto Sunnyside and proceed to the end.

o   Cross Deer Valley Drive, turn right and proceed through three crosswalks at the roundabout.

o   Bear right out of the roundabout and quickly turn left onto the Poison Creek Trail. After Shoetree Park, ascend stairs by a fire hydrant.

- Bus riders turn left onto Main Street and follow it to the Main and 9th Streets intersection.
- Turn right on 9th Street and follow it to Park Avenue for a bus stop.
- Drivers turn right, cross Main Street and proceed to Deer Valley Drive.
- Turn left onto Deer Valley Drive and cross it at the intersection with Aerie Drive.

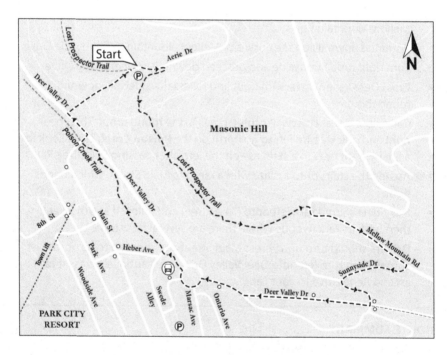

#4 Masonic Hill – Deer Valley

#5 Ontario Ridge – Rossie Hill

DESCRIPTION: This route starts and ends in Old Town, takes you along ridgeline trails through mossy woodlands, and offers a peek into Park City's unpolished past.

Distance: 2.5 miles (4 km)

Elevation Gain: 397 feet (121 m)

Peak Elevation: 7,586 feet (2312 m)

Difficulty: DIFFICULT due to a steep ascent for the first 1/4 mile (0.4 km) and descent on narrow single-track.

Surface: Mostly dirt with pavement and staircases mixed in.

Restrooms are not available along this route. **Detour** to Main Street (see Walk #1).

NOTABLE FEATURES:

◊ **Prospect Avenue** features historic residences and some vestiges of old Park City are found along the **Prospect Trail** on Ontario Ridge.

◊ The City purchased land here for trail preservation. **Trail connections** are available.

DIRECTIONS:

- Take the Main Street **Trolley** to the turnaround where Main Street intersects with Hillside Avenue. Proceed east, ascending Hillside to Prospect Avenue and turn right on Prospect.

- **Drivers** can park in the Sandridge two-tiered lot, accessible from Deer Valley Drive at the south end of Old Town. Find a sidewalk in the southwest corner of the upper lot and follow it to Hillside Avenue. Cross Hillside to get to Prospect Avenue

- Ascend on Prospect to a dirt trail at the top. (Prospect Ave then goes downhill to the left. Limited parking here was not recommended to avoid the steep climb at the route's end.)

- Proceed onto the **Prospect Trail** and follow it south to a three-pronged fork.

- Take the middle branch and arrive at a second fork.

- Bear left to descend on a narrow trail from Ontario Ridge to Marsac Avenue.

- Carefully cross Marsac and turn right. Pass a steep gravel road and find a dirt path to your left, the **Rossie Hill Trail**.

- Turn sharply left onto this trail and follow it as it bends. Ignore a left switchback and then ignore a right fork. Arrive at a double-track dirt road.

- Turn left onto this road and come to an intersection of multiple trails. Take the trail to the right, passing two low boulders to your left.

- Ignore the first right turn and take the second right turn onto another single-track, which ends on a paved cul-de-sac, McHenry Avenue. Walk north on McHenry to a long staircase on the left.

- Descend the stairs and turn right onto Ontario Avenue. Walk north on Ontario to another long staircase on the left.

- Descend these stairs to Marsac Avenue. Cross Marsac, take a few steps down and turn left onto a sidewalk that circles a pocket park. **Bus** riders should follow the pocket park path to the right to Swede Alley. Turn right on Swede to get to the transit center.

- **Drivers** take the pocket park circular sidewalk to the left to a staircase to the lower Sandridge parking. There are more stairs to the upper lot.

ROUTE SUMMARY:

o   Start at Prospect Avenue, at the south end of Old Town.

o   Ascend the steep road to the top and continue onto the Prospect Trail.

o   At a three-pronged fork, take the middle branch and come to a second fork.

o   Bear left onto a narrow trail down to Marsac Avenue.

o   Cross Marsac, turn right, pass a gravel road and turn sharply left onto single-track. Ignore a left switchback and a right fork. Come to double-track road.

o   Turn left and come to an intersection.

o   Bear right at the intersection, passing low boulders to the left.

o   Pass a right turn and turn right at a second intersecting trail. Follow it to a cul-de-sac and continue on the street to a staircase to the left.

o   Take the stairs down, turn right, and proceed to the next staircase on the left.

o   Take the stairs down to Marsac Avenue and cross it. Descend more stairs and turn left onto a circular sidewalk. Bus riders turn right to get to Swede Alley and the transit center.

o   Drivers turn left and the circular sidewalk arrives at a staircase that ascends to the Sandridge parking lots.

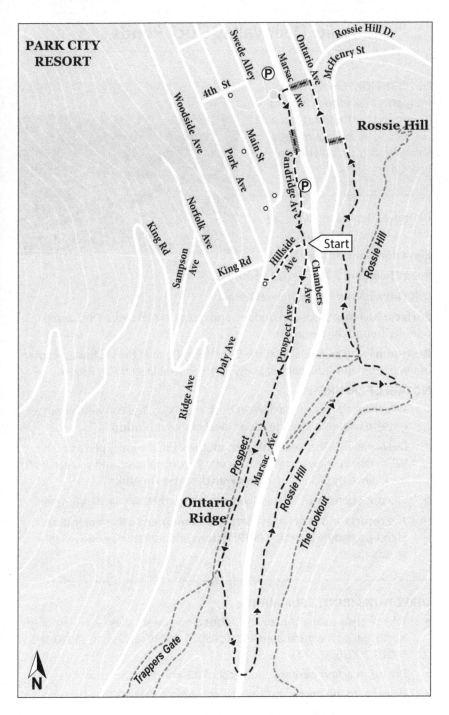

PARK CITY RESORT

Swede Alley

4th St

Woodside Ave

Main St

Park Ave

Norfolk Ave

King Rd

Sampson Ave

King Rd

Ridge Ave

Daly Ave

Prospect Ave

Hillside Ave

Sandridge Ave

Marsac Ave

Ontario Ave

McHenry St

Rossie Hill Dr

Rossie Hill

Rossie Hill

Start

Chambers Ave

Prospect

Marsac Ave

Rossie Hill

The Lookout

Ontario Ridge

Trappers Gate

N

#5 Ontario Ridge – Rossie Hill

#6 Deer Valley Duck Ponds

DESCRIPTION: Enjoy a maze of footpaths meandering around ponds and posh condos in a park like setting at the foot of Deer Valley Resort, a subdivision of Park City.

Distance: Depending on route, 1 to 1.5 miles (1.6-2.4 km)

Elevation Gain: 46 feet (14 m)

Peak Elevation: 7,203 feet (21.95m)

Difficulty: EASY walking on level terrain.

Surface: Pavement, wooden bridges, and dirt or gravel paths. Find paved options around the periphery.

Restrooms may be available at the Deer Valley Plaza at the southwest corner of the ponds, and seasonally at Snow Park Lodge at Deer Valley Resort.

NOTABLE FEATURES:

◊ **Wildlife** may come for a drink at dusk and dawn. You can watch from a **gazebo** within this refuge. It's an ideal place for **birding**.

◊ **Detour** to ride the **free funicular**, southeast of the entry plaza to Deer Valley Resort. Views from the funicular are outstanding and you can walk back down by picking up **Finn's Trail** described in Walk #7.

◊ The duck pond walks are easily **combined** with Walks #4, #7, #8, or #9.

◊ The **resorts** and Deer Valley Plaza offer **dining**, and other **amenities**. Stand-up paddle boarding (**SUP**) lessons and rentals may be available seasonally.

DIRECTIONS (ROUTE SUMMARY):

▪ Take the **bus** to any of many bus stops along Deer Valley Drive East or North. (Stops are numbered 45010, 45020, 45030, etc., up to 45090, then, 50010, 50020, 50030.)

▪ Drivers may find **parking** southeast of the ponds in the resort lots.

▪ Have fun in the **maze**. You'll always come out on Deer Valley Drive near a bus stop if you get disoriented.

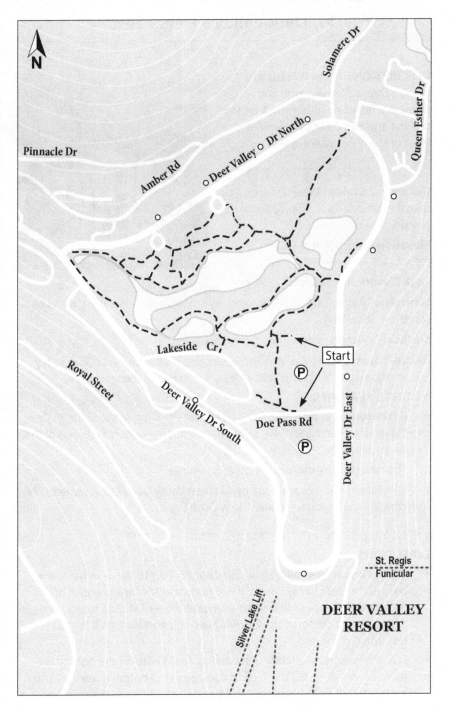

#6 Deer Valley Duck Ponds

#7 Deer Valley – Deer Crest

DESCRIPTION: This walk takes you along a Deer Valley ski slope and through a resort neighborhood. Riding the St. Regis Funicular can eliminate most of the uphill walking.

Distance: 2.5 miles (4 km) if you don't take the funicular, 1.8 miles (2.9 km) if you do.

Elevation Gain: 394 feet (120 m) for walkers

Peak Elevation: 7,508 feet (2,288 m)

Difficulty: EASY or DIFFICULT, depending on use of the funicular. Drivers have some uphill walking.

Surface: Pavement, single-track trails, and stairs.

Restrooms may be available at Snow Park Lodge at the base of Deer Valley Resort seasonally, or at Deer Valley Plaza, southwest of the resort.

NOTABLE FEATURES:

◊ A **free funicular ride** goes from Deer Valley parking to the St. Regis Deer Valley Resort and back. The Swiss-made tram provides great views of the ski slopes and duck ponds.

◊ The **resorts** offer **dining** and other amenities.

◊ There are numerous **trail options** at Deer Valley Resort. This route easily combines with route #6 Deer Valley Duck Ponds.

DIRECTIONS:

▪ Start at **bus stop 45090**, *Snow Park Lodge & Deer Valley*, or **drive** to the base of the Deer Valley Resort. If you park near the funicular east of the resort base, some uphill walking comes at the end of the route. Parking in the northeast corner of the lots will have you walking uphill to start with less uphill at the end.

▪ From the resort base looking at parking, find a road on the right to the funicular building. On the second floor, push the button if the funicular car is not there. On top of the tracks, exit the building to the southeast, opposite the duck ponds.

- To walk instead of ride, look for **Finn's Trail** to your left, as soon as you turn onto the road to the funicular building.
- Turn left onto Finn's Trail. Follow it to an intersection where you'll turn right at a switchback. Come to a T-intersection.
- Turn left and come to another intersection (switchback).
- Turn right to merge with the **St. Regis Connector Trail**. Come to another intersection.
- Turn right. Cross under the funicular to arrive at the upper funicular building.
- From the south side of the building, continue past the resort pools onto a ski slope. As the slope descends under a road, bear left and take a few steps up to the resort plaza.
- Turn right and follow the plaza around the periphery of the resort to a staircase.
- Descend these stairs and turn left onto a road, Deer Crest Estates Drive.
- Proceed downhill on Deer Crest. Come to gates that allow passage around the sides. Arrive at a second set of gates after a short distance. Pass around either side to follow a dirt path that ends on Queen Esther Drive.
- Turn left on Queen Esther and proceed to Deer Valley Drive East.
- Turn left on Deer Valley Drive East to get the **car**. **Bus** stops are to the right or left.

ROUTE SUMMARY:

o   Start at the east end of the Deer Valley Resort base where a road ascends to a funicular building for the option of an uphill lift.

o   Walkers turn left onto Finn's Trail at the start of the road to the funicular.

o   Walking up Finn's trail, you'll come to four intersections. Turn right at the first, left at the second, and turn right at the third and fourth.

o   From the top funicular building, bear left around the resort pools, arriving at three steps.

o   Ascend to a plaza and bear right to a staircase.

o   Descend the stairs and turn left, heading north on Deer Crest Estates Drive. Pass around two sets of gates to descend onto a dirt path that ends on Queen Esther Drive.

o   Turn left on Queen Esther and proceed to Deer Valley Drive East.

o   Turn left onto Deer Valley Drive to return to parking, or right for the closest bus stop.

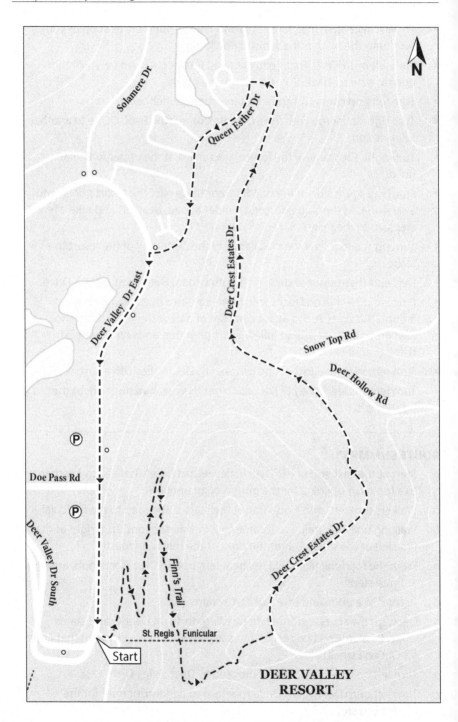

#7 Deer Valley – Deer Crest

#8 Silver Lake Village

DESCRIPTION: This is a short, easy walk amidst the glitz and glamour of Deer Valley Resort. Seasonal chair lift access provides additional options.

Distance: 1.2 miles (1.9 km)

Elevation Gain: 43 feet (13 m)

Peak Elevation: 8,175 feet (2,492 m)

Difficulty: EASY. Inclines are gentle. This is the highest altitude walk in this book.

Surface: Sidewalk and paved roads.

Restrooms may be available seasonally in the Silver Lake Lodge.

NOTABLE FEATURES:

◊ **Silver Lake Village** is the midsection of Deer Valley Resort. Stores, restaurants, and chairlifts operate seasonally. **Cyclists** careening down ski slopes entertain the lunch crowd. Chairlift access to Deer Valley's cycling can create long lift lines, as seen in this photo.

◊ Woodland View Drive passes through a **mountain pine forest** where mansions capture exceptional views.

◊ Summer **resort activities** include concerts, special events, access to numerous trails, and chairlift rides to higher elevations. (*deervalley.com*)

DIRECTIONS (ROUTE SUMMARY):

- Service to the Silver Lake Village **bus stop** may only be available during summer and ski seasons. **Drivers** could take Royal Street to Silver Lake, but free parking is hard to come by and fees can be steep. Walking up to Silver Lake is possible but a lack of shoulders on winding Royal Street makes it risky. The bus is the best option when available.

- From the bus stop or parking, head east onto Royal Street East. It bends left and takes you past Sterling Drive to Woodland View Drive.

- Turn left on Woodland View and follow it to Royal Street.

- Turn left on Royal Street, cross to the sidewalk, and follow it back to the **bus** stop or **parking**.

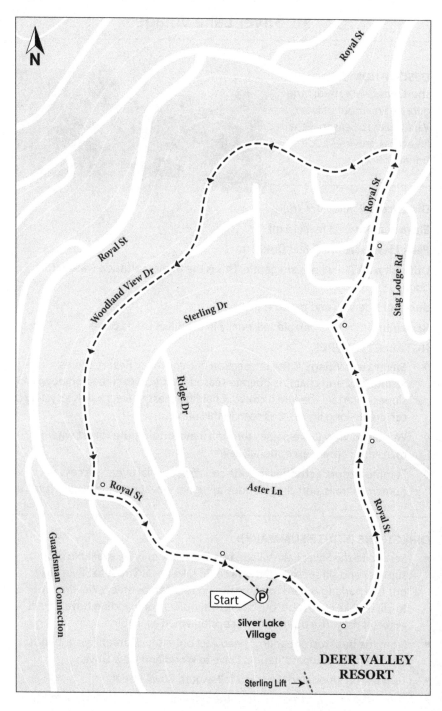

#8 Silver Lake Village

#9 Lower and Upper Deer Valley

DESCRIPTION: Neighborhood walks are a great hiking alternative when mountain trails are snowy. This route takes you past some of Park City's most palatial properties.

Distance: 4.8 miles (7.7 km)
Elevation Gain: 387 feet (186 m)
Peak Elevation: 7,402 feet or (2,256 m)
Difficulty: INTERMEDIATE. Although you'll climb for long distance, the inclines are gentle.

Surface: This walk can be completed on pavement, but directions include some off-road.

Restrooms may be available only at the start and end of this loop at Deer Valley Plaza, or seasonally at Snow Park Lodge. Be prepared.

NOTABLE FEATURES:

◊ Outstanding **views** will greet you going and coming. Homes are set in parks with pedestrian paths and ponds, and along mountain ridges.

◊ This walk is easily **combined** with Walks #6 or #7.

◊ Dining may be available seasonally at the **resorts** and at Deer Valley Plaza year-round.

DIRECTIONS:

- **Bus stop 45060** *Queen Esther & Deer Valley Drive* leaves you on Deer Valley Drive East. Walk south to Queen Esther Drive and turn left.
- **Drivers** may park in the northeast corner of the northern resort parking lot. Walk north on Deer Valley Drive East to Queen Esther Drive and turn right.
- Follow Queen Esther around to an intersection with Telemark Drive.
- Turn right on Telemark and ascend to Thistle Street.
- Turn right on Thistle and proceed to Sunridge Drive.
- Turn right on Sunridge and proceed to Hidden Oaks Lane.
- Turn left on Hidden Oaks and proceed to Solamere Drive.

- Turn left on Solamere and follow it to a left turn marked "Northern Entrance to Telemark Drive" and turn left. (To avoid unpaved walking, do not take the entrance to Telemark but continue down Solamere to Deer Valley Drive and back to start.)
- If you turned left on Telemark, proceed a short way to find a gravel path on the right.
- Turn right onto this path, which turns into sidewalk. Follow it around tennis courts. Come to a fork near a pond.
- Take either of the paths around the pond to return to Queen Esther Drive.
- Turn right on Queen Esther and proceed to Deer Valley Drive.
- Turn right to return to the **bus** or left to return to **parking**.

ROUTE SUMMARY:

o Start on Queen Esther Drive walking uphill.

o Turn right on Telemark Drive.

o Turn right on Thistle Street.

o Turn right on Sunridge Drive.

o Turn left on Hidden Oaks Lane.

o Turn left on Solamere Drive.

o Turn left at the sign "Northern Entrance to Telemark Drive".

o Turn right onto a gravel path. Follow it to sidewalk and come to a fork at a pond.

o Take either path around the pond to Queen Esther Drive and turn right. Proceed to Deer Valley Drive.

o Turn right on Deer Valley Drive for the bus or left for parking.

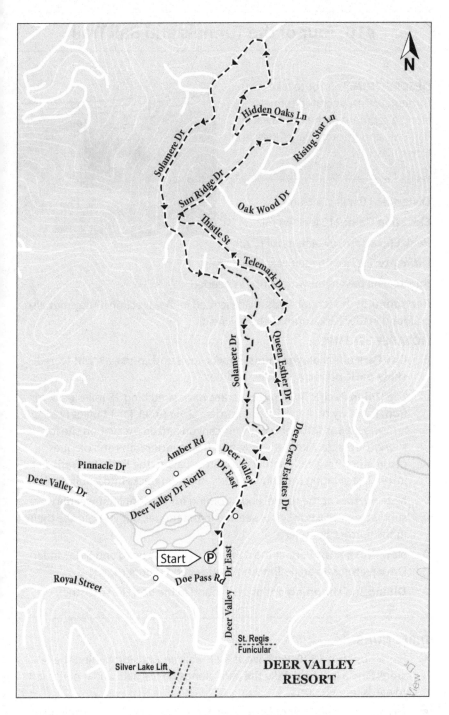

#9 Lower and Upper Deer Valley

#10 Tour of the Tunnels and Rail Trail

DESCRIPTION: This route takes you through artist-decorated tunnels, along a segment of the Union Pacific Rail Trail, and through Park City's "Iron Horse" District.

Distance: 3.0 miles (4.8 km)

Elevation Gain: 210 feet (64 m)

Peak Elevation: 6,924 feet (2,110 m)

Difficulty: EASY with relatively level terrain.

Surface: All pavement with ramps as needed.

Restrooms at the school fields are described in the directions. They may also be found in City Park, south of the ball fields.

NOTABLE FEATURES:

◊ **City Park** offers **playgrounds, sports** fields and courts, a multi-teared **skate park**, **picnic**, and other facilities.

◊ The **Union Pacific Rail Trail** is a **state park** stretching 28 miles (45 km) from Park City north to Echo. It borders Silver Creek for 14 miles (22.5 km) and passes through a volcanic canyon and an excavation site for Ice Age artifacts. Along the way, find **trail connections** and plaques commemorating early settlers. Congress passed the **Rails-To-Trails Act** in 1983, facilitating the conversion of idle train tracks into public trails.

◊ Note **mirrors** at the tunnel ends. Coming from bright light wearing sunglasses, cyclists may not see you in the tunnel, but you can see them in the mirrors. Stay alert.

◊ **New Prospector Park** at the corner of Comstock Road and Sidewinder Drive features an arch-**climbing boulder** and fountains.

◊ **Dining** and **shopping** options are found in the Iron Horse District.

DIRECTIONS:

▪ From **bus stop 1520**, *Park Ave at 7-11*, walk around and behind the 7-11 store. Find a ball field. Take the path alongside the field and it bends left towards tennis courts.

▪ **Drivers** turn south off of Deer Valley Drive and park at the north end of City Park near the tennis courts.

- Take the paved path right of the tennis courts to another path, the **Poison Creek Trail.**
- Turn left onto Poison Creek. Follow it through a short and a long tunnel.
- After the second tunnel, turn right onto the blacktop path just before a clock tower. This is the **Rail Trail**. Proceed about 2/3 of a mile (1.06 km) to the **Kearns Bike Path**.
- Turn left. Follow this paved path through a parking lot to Sidewinder Drive. New Prospector Park is to the right.
- Cross Sidewinder and continue north on the sidewalk along Comstock Road to a traffic light at Kearns Boulevard.
- Take the stairs or ramp on the right to a tunnel that takes you under Kearns.
- Bear left out of the tunnel. Follow the sidewalk as it jigs around a road divider. Continue along Kearns Boulevard passing the schools. (Just east of the high school parking is a path to a ball field and a small building with public restrooms.) Continue west along Kearns to the intersection of Kearns, Monitor, and Bonanza Drives.
- Using crosswalks, first cross Monitor and then cross Kearns.
- Follow the sidewalk on the west side of Bonanza Drive. It crosses Iron Horse Drive and merges with the Poison Creek Trail back to City Park.
- Turn right past the tennis courts to arrive back at the **parking**.
- **Bus** riders turn left after the courts to return to the bus stop in front of the 7-11 store.

ROUTE SUMMARY:

o Start on a path in the north end of City Park next to tennis courts.

o Pass the courts and turn left onto an intersecting path. Proceed through two tunnels and come to a clock tower.

o Turn right onto the Rail Trail and proceed 2/3 mile (1.06 km) to the Kearns Bike Path.

o Turn left, cross Sidewinder Drive and proceed north along Comstock Road.

o Take the tunnel under Kearns Boulevard and bear left upon exit. Follow the sidewalk along Kearns Boulevard to Monitor Drive.

o Cross Monitor Drive and then cross Kearns Boulevard.

o Proceed along Bonanza Drive. It crosses Iron Horse Drive and merges with the Poison Creek Trail.

o Proceed to City Park and turn right past the tennis courts to return to start.

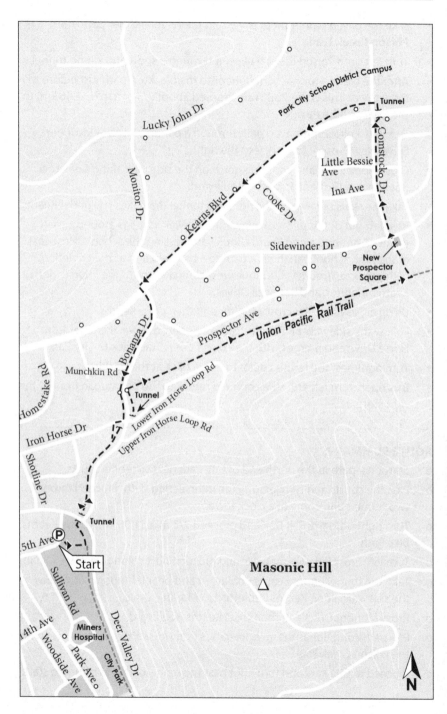

#10 Tour of the Tunnels and Rail Trail

#11 Olympic Plaza – Kearns Boulevard

DESCRIPTION: This suburban route takes you from Olympic glory to public-school ball fields where future Olympians may be starting careers. More than 60 U.S.A. athletes competing in the 2014 Sochi Olympics lived/trained in Park City.

This route also provides a poignant perspective on local history. The skier headstone in this photo leaves little doubt that some in repose in the Park City Cemetery would appreciate their perpetual mountain view.

Distance: 2.9 miles (4.7 km)

Elevation Gain: 98 feet (30 m)

Peak Elevation: 6,838 feet (2084 m)

Difficulty: This is an EASY level walk.

Surface: All paved except for a few steps on a dirt footpath.

Restrooms may be accessible at businesses and alongside the high school ball fields.

NOTABLE FEATURES:

◊ **Snow Creek Shopping Center**, the **Holiday Village Shopping Center**, and other commercial properties along this route offer stores, restaurants, movie theaters, professional services, and other amenities. A **commemorative bell** at the Holiday Village Shopping Center offers a vignette of the lives of early settlers.

◊ **Olympic Welcome Plaza** is a pocket park that honors athletes of the 2002 Salt Lake City Olympics, and Olympic venues around the world. You can snap a selfie on the gold, silver, or bronze podium.

◊ **Park City Cemetery** was established in the latter 1800s when the first settlers buried a daughter, Pearl Snyder. Also interred here is Rachel Urban. (Read about this infamous madam in this book's chapter, "Park City's Colorful Past.") A gazebo provides shade, seating, and a map to sections for firefighters, veterans, and other congregations.

◊ Around the **schools**, find full-sized and small baseball **fields**, a softball field, and a turf field that triples for football, soccer and lacrosse, an outdoor track, and a **playground**.

◊ Find **connecting paths** around Treasure Mountain Junior High where there are additional ball fields, a creek, and a path accessing wetlands, as described in Walk #18.

◊ Route 248 is named after **Thomas Kearns**, who started out as a mucker in the mines and studied geology at night. He discovered rich veins of ore and became an owner of the lucrative Silver King Mine. In addition to becoming a banking, railroad, and newspaper magnate, he served as a United States senator (1901-05).

◊ This route easily **combines** with #12 Boot Hill - McLeod Creek.

DIRECTIONS:

▪ Ride to **bus stop 1900**, *Park Ave at Squatters*. Walk south on Park, turn left onto Kearns Boulevard, and quickly turn left onto a paved path into the Olympic Welcome Plaza. You will exit the plaza on the opposite side.

▪ **Parking** is available for shoppers only at Snow Creek Shopping Center on the northeast corner of the T-intersection of Park Avenue (Rt. 224) and Kearns Boulevard (Rt. 248).

▪ From shopping, cross the street behind the liquor store (identifiable by signage on its side). To your immediate left is a sidewalk that takes you into the Olympic Welcome Plaza. Exit the plaza the same way you came in.

▪ From the north exit of the Olympic Plaza, turn right onto the sidewalk going east. Cross a shopping center entry road. Continue along Kearns Boulevard. The Park City Cemetery fence appears on the left.

▪ Turn into the first cemetery gate. Follow the paths turning left at intersections. (Hopefully, you are not avoidant of cemeteries; they provide insight into the history of a place and its people not found elsewhere. You can however, walk alongside the cemetery by staying on the Kearns sidewalk.) If you've come through the cemetery, you'll ultimately arrive at a dirt footpath next to the cemetery fence that takes you to Monitor Drive.

▪ Turn right onto Monitor and proceed to the traffic light. Cross Monitor and continue east along Kearns. Pass the high school parking lots. Continue on the sidewalk as it jigs left and right around parking, and becomes blacktop leading to the ball fields. (Restrooms are available in the small building between the ball fields.) Past the restrooms, the sidewalk turns right and continues into the parking lot of McPolin Elementary School.

- Turn left into the parking lot next to a playground and immediately turn left again onto blacktop that goes behind the high school. You'll be heading west alongside of Lucky John Drive, with which the path will merge. Continue on Lucky John Drive to Monitor Drive.

- Turn left onto Monitor and continue south to the traffic light. You now have options:
  ◊ Cross Monitor and go back through the cemetery, or walk alongside the cemetery to return to start
  ◊ Cross Kearns and turn right onto the sidewalk where you'll have dining and shopping options. This is the recommended route, but you'll need to cross Kearns again at the T-intersection of Routes 224 and 248.

- **Bus** riders proceed along 224, Park Avenue, for the bus stop.

- **Drivers** immediately turn right onto sidewalk and then turn left into and through the Olympic Welcome Plaza to the Snow Creek Shopping Center.

ROUTE SUMMARY:

o   Start at the Olympic Welcome Plaza in the southwest corner of the Snow Creek shopping plaza. Exit the Welcome Plaza to the north and turn right. Follow this sidewalk along Kearns Boulevard to the first gate of the cemetery.

o   Turn left into the cemetery and follow paths taking left turns. Come to a dirt road just north of the cemetery fence. Exit the cemetery by turning right onto Monitor Drive.

o   Proceed south on Monitor to the traffic light. Cross Monitor and follow the sidewalk along Kearns, passing the school parking. At the McPolin School playground, find a sidewalk.

o   Turn left and follow this sidewalk. It merges with Lucky John Drive. Proceed west on Lucky John to Monitor Drive.

o   Turn left onto Monitor and proceed to the traffic light. Cross to the south side of Kearns and turn right, following the paved path going west to the T-intersection of Park Avenue and Kearns.

o   Cross to the north side of the T-intersection. Bus riders find your stop on Park Avenue.

o   Drivers turn right and then left onto sidewalk into and through the Olympic Welcome Plaza back to start.

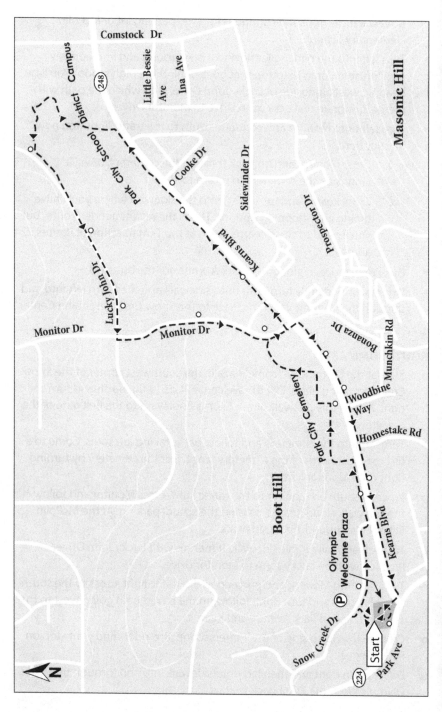

#11 Olympic Plaza – Kearns Boulevard

#12 Boot Hill – McLeod Creek

DESCRIPTION: Climb a little hill with big views on your way to shop or dine. This short route also takes you on a paved trail through protected wetlands.

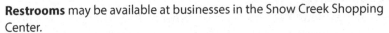

Distance: 1 mile (1.6 km)

Elevation Gain: 31 feet (9.4 m)

Peak Elevation: 6,854 feet (2,089 m)

Difficulty: INTERMEDIATE due to a moderately steep start.

Surface: Gravelly dirt single-track with ribbons of old asphalt leads to pavement.

Restrooms may be available at businesses in the Snow Creek Shopping Center.

NOTABLE FEATURES:

◊ The **views** of Park City and Deer Valley Resorts from easy access **Boot Hill** are grand. This is a perfect perch for watching **sunsets** with adequate light to safely descend.

◊ The paved path along the **McLeod** (pronounced ma-cloud) **Creek Trail** traverses a riparian buffer zone where **beaver dams** preserve water quality by filtering out pollution. This stream feeds into the Weber River Watershed which provides drinking water for multiple Wasatch Front municipalities.

◊ You could **detour** to see the **Olympic Welcome Plaza**, featured in Walk #11.

DIRECTIONS:

- Ride to **bus stop 1900**, *Park Ave at Squatters*. Walk south on Park, turn left onto Kearns Boulevard, and immediately turn left onto a paved path through the Olympic Welcome Plaza. Exit the plaza on the opposite side and cross the street into the parking areas.

- **Parking** is available only for customers of the Snow Creek Shopping Center on the northeast corner of the intersection of Park Avenue (Rt. 224) and Kearns Boulevard (Rt. 248).

- From the northeast corner of the shopping center, cross the road towards Zions Bank and turn left onto a sidewalk. At the end of the sidewalk, turn left onto a gravel road and proceed through a few switchbacks. Find a fork to the left just as you are in line with the northwest corner of the big building below you.
- Bear left and follow this path until it ends on blacktop.
- Turn right onto the blacktop path and immediately turn left onto Saddle View Way, descending amidst townhomes to Windrift Lane.
- Turn left onto a path on the west side of Windrift, bordering an office park. This is the **McLeod Creek Trail** which goes back to the Snow Creek Shopping Center.
- From **parking**, **bus** riders should walk through the Olympic Welcome Plaza just south of the liquor store and turn right twice for the bus stop on Route 224.

ROUTE SUMMARY:

o   Start at the sidewalk at the northeast corner of the Snow Creek Shopping Center. It becomes a gravel path. Continue on this path through switchbacks to a fork.

o   Bear left at the fork and follow this dirt path to a blacktop path.

o   Turn right and immediately turn left onto Saddle View Way. Proceed to Windrift Lane.

o   Turn left onto the path west of Windrift. Follow it back to the shopping center.

o   Walk through Olympic Plaza and turn right twice for the bus.

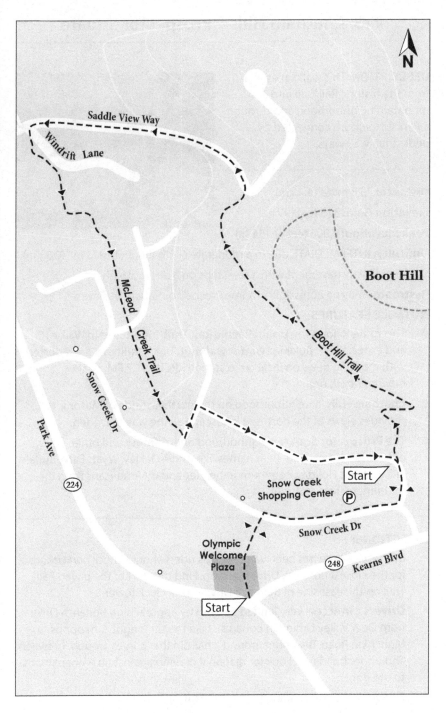

#12 Boot Hill – McLeod Creek

#13 Chatham Hills – Prospector Square

DESCRIPTION: This walk takes you from the historic Rail Trail into a mountain neighborhood and through a Park City suburb connected by pedestrian walkways.

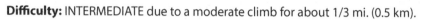

Distance: 2.75 miles (4.4 km)

Elevation Gain: 318 feet (97 m)

Peak Elevation: 7,006 feet (2,135 m)

Difficulty: INTERMEDIATE due to a moderate climb for about 1/3 mi. (0.5 km).

Surface: Mostly pavement with a few steps on a dirt footpath.

Restrooms may be accessible in some Prospector Square businesses.

NOTABLE FEATURES:

◊ This route follows the **Union Pacific Rail Trail**, introduced in Walk #10 and especially popular for **winter walking**. Trail conditions are reported with morning news on local radio station KPCW, 91.7 FM, or at *mountaintrails.org*.

◊ **Chatham Hills**, a neighborhood on the northeast side of Masonic Hill, provides views of the northern landscape all the way to Ogden.

◊ The **Prospector Square** neighborhood offers **dining** and other enterprise. Streets here bear names like Annie Oakley, Wyatt Earp, Buffalo Bill, and Doc Holiday, commemorating legendary Americans from the mid-nineteenth century.

DIRECTIONS:

- Bus service here has been variable. **Bus** riders should check *parkcity.org* for the closest Bonanza Drive bus stop. Find the start of the paved Rail Trail on the east side of Bonanza Drive near a clock tower.

- **Drivers** can access very limited parking by approaching Bonanza Drive from Deer Valley Drive. On Bonanza, take the third right turn opposite Munchkin Road. Bear right around a hairpin that curves around, between and under buildings. Look for diagonal parking against an embankment to the right.

- Find a footpath ascending to the **Rail Trail** and turn left.

- Follow the Rail Trail heading east, ignoring the first three trail connections on the right. Come to a sign for the **Gambel Oak Trail** on the right.
- Turn right onto this short footpath and then cross paved Paddington Drive. Continue straight onto Euston Drive, walking uphill. Just before Euston ends, come to an intersection with (upper) Paddington Drive.
- Turn right onto Paddington. Continue uphill until you come to High Street.
- Turn left onto High Street. Follow it around a horseshoe back to Paddington.
- Turn left onto Paddington. Continue downhill until the road bends right. Look for a footpath straight ahead before the bend and take it back to the Rail Trail.
- Turn left onto the Rail Trail. Quickly come to a right turn marked **Kearns Bike Path**.
- Turn right and follow this path past storage facilities. Come out in a parking lot and find a sidewalk to the left between buildings.
- Turn left onto this sidewalk. Cross more parking lots and paved Gold Dust and Poison Creek Lanes. Continue into a plaza with restaurants. Follow the sidewalk as it bends left and arrives on Prospector Drive. Bus service might be available on Prospector by turning left, or cross Prospector Drive and proceed through a commercial parking lot to find a footpath back onto the Rail Trail.
- Turn right onto the Rail Trail to return to a Bonanza Drive **bus stop** or **parking**.

ROUTE SUMMARY:

o Start at the Rail Trail's west end near the clock tower east of Bonanza Drive.

o Proceed east on the Rail Trail past three trail intersection to arrive at the Gambel Oak Trail intersection.

o Turn right onto a dirt footpath.

o Cross Paddington Drive and walk up Euston Drive.

o Turn right onto (upper) Paddington Drive.

o Turn left onto High Street.

o Turn left onto Paddington Drive (again) and find a footpath just before the road bends right. Take the footpath back to the Rail Trail.

o Turn left onto the Rail Trail. Come to an intersecting trail.

o Turn right onto the Kearns Bike Path. Pass a storage area, come to a parking lot and find a sidewalk to your left between buildings.

o Turn left onto this sidewalk and continue on it, crossing streets, through a plaza, and around a bend to Prospector Avenue.

o Cross the street, proceed through a commercial parking lot to arrive at a foot path back to the Rail Trail.

o Turn right onto the Rail Trail to return to parking or Bonanza Drive for the bus.

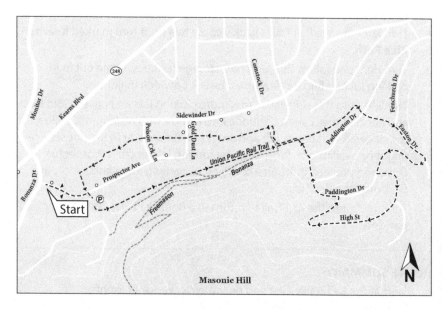

#13 Chatham Hills – Prospector Square

#14 Thaynes Canyon

DESCRIPTION: This route meanders around the municipal golf course and takes you through a neighborhood nestled at the base of ski terrain. The contrast between old and new mountain architecture is striking in this older Park City suburb.

Distance: 2.4 miles (3.8 kg)

Elevation Gain: 200 feet (61 m)

Peak Elevation: 6,918 feet (2,128 m)

Difficulty: INTERMEDIATE: A few short, steep inclines and a long gentle incline at the end.

Surface: Pavement, and a few steps on dirt footpaths.

Restrooms may be available at the Park City and Silver Star Resorts and the Hotel Park City golf/ski clubhouse.

NOTABLE FEATURES:

◊ Park City **Municipal Golf Course** becomes the **White Pine Nordic Touring Center** in winter, with groomed trails for classic and skate skiing. This wonderfully walkable mountain golf course features water on eleven holes, making it a wildlife oasis.

◊ The **Glenwood Cemetery** was established in 1885 and is still in use. Avoid touching the fragile sandstone grave markers.

◊ **Silver Star Plaza** is a ski in/out resort offering lodging, **dining**, **retail**, **concerts**, **trail access** and more. Note the **Spiro Tunnel** as you exit the plaza. Drainage tunnels under the mountains were constructed to rid the mines of water. Before ski lifts were built, skiers rode a mine train through this tunnel to a hoist which lifted them up the mountain. In 2020, Spiro tunnel entrance came under construction.

◊ **Park City Resort** amenities, as described in Walks #2 and #3 are also accessible.

DIRECTIONS:

- **Bus stop 1000**, *PC Mountain*, takes you to the resort base and possible **parking**.
- In the northwest corner of the parking area near the First Time chairlift, descend on a short footpath to a sidewalk along condos to the right. Follow this sidewalk to the road. The Glenwood Cemetery is to the left. Enter to the right of the gate.
- If you've skipped or exited the cemetery, follow Silver King Drive to Three Kings Drive.
- Turn left on Three Kings and proceed north to Crescent Ridge Road.
- Turn left onto Crescent Ridge. Ascend to find a pedestrian path forking right, as the road bends left.
- Turn right and proceed on the footpath towards the chairlift. Pass through the plaza to arrive on Three Kings Drive.
- Turn left onto Three Kings and proceed to a four-way intersection.
- Turn right onto Thaynes Canyon Drive. Beware of errant golf balls from the driving range to the right. After passing Hotel Park City, find a paved path bordering Route 224.
- Turn right onto this path and proceed until it ends at Silver King Drive.
- Cross Silver King to another sidewalk.
- Turn right to return to resort **parking** or the **bus**.

ROUTE SUMMARY:

- Start in the northwest corner of the Park City Resort parking near the First Time chairlift.
- Take a dirt footpath to the sidewalk north of the chairlifts and follow the sidewalk to a road and Glenwood Cemetery.
- Upon exiting the cemetery, follow Silver King Drive east to Three Kings Drive.
- Turn left onto Three Kings and proceed to Crescent Ridge Road.
- Ascend Crescent Ridge and turn right onto a path where the road bends left.
- Proceed through the Silver Star Plaza back to Three Kings Drive.
- Turn left onto Three Kings and proceed to a 4-way intersection.
- Turn right onto Thaynes Canyon Drive and proceed to the end.
- Turn right onto a path along Route 224 and continue to it end.
- Cross Silver King Drive and turn right to return to the bus or parking.

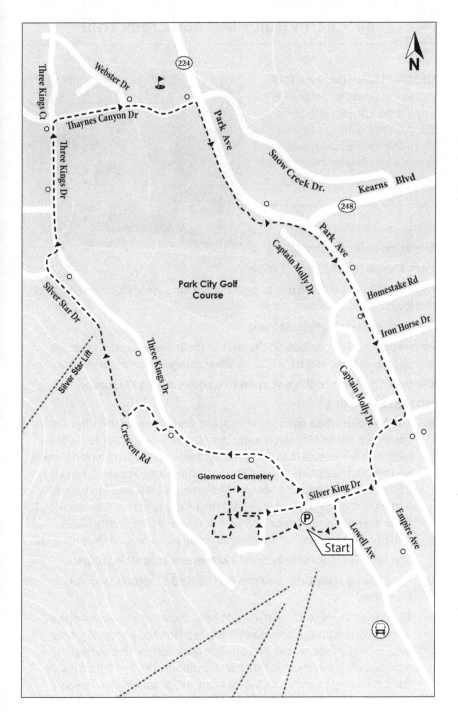

#14 Thaynes Canyon

#15 Farm Trail – McLeod Creek Trail

DESCRIPTION: The paved trails of this route take you along Park City's entry corridor and through the property of the iconic McPolin barn. The trails follow streams and provide benches for taking in the views.

Distance: 3.5 miles (5.6 km)

Elevation Gain: 148 feet (45 m)

Peak Elevation: 6,825 feet (2,080 m)

Difficulty: INTERMEDIATE due to a gentle but long ascent for the first half of this loop.

Surface: All paved paths and roads.

Restrooms may be available in the back of the building northwest of the McPolin barn, at the Hotel Park City golf/ski clubhouse, or at some businesses.

Caution: The **Farm Trail is not open to walkers during ski season**.

NOTABLE FEATURES:

◊ The **McPolin white barn** beckons artists and photographers from around the world. Daniel McPolin bought the 80-acre farm in 1897 for $600 to help feed early settlers. In 1908, the barn was built with recycled timbers and without nails. Veterinarian Dr. D.A. Osguthorpe acquired the farm in 1947. When Route 224 became four lanes in 1990, and too busy for a cattle crossing, Dr. Osguthorpe sold the property to Park City Municipal for **preserved open space**. The barn serves as a community facility. Vintage farm equipment is displayed along paths around the buildings.

◊ The Farm Trail traditionally hosts a **scarecrow contest** in autumn.

◊ A metal ring **sculpture** at a Farm Trail trailhead captures views of Olympic ski slopes.

◊ **Richards Ranch**, south of the white barn, provides 20-acres of **open space** where horses often roam. Protected land has historically been supported by federal laws that provide tax credit for landowners who donate property or sell it at an affordable price to a land trust for community benefit. Landowners can also acquire conservation easements by retaining their land in an undeveloped state. The Summit

Land Conservancy, private citizens, and voters have helped preserve precious Park City property, as seen in this walk. Find information about protected lands at *wesaveland.org*.

◊ The paved trail along **McLeod Creek** is ideal for birding and observing beaver activity. Beavers dam up streams to create predator-safe moats around their homes. A beaver lodge has a foyer to dry off in and a ventilated room on top for the beaver family to sleep and play in. It's unlikely you'll see the beavers though. These aquatic athletes mostly work the night shift. Beaver ponds create habitat for other wildlife and purify stream water.

◊ You might observe extreme human athletes tumbling through the air in the **jump bike park** along the McLeod Creek Trail.

◊ **Snow Creek Shopping Center** provides shopping and dining options.

DIRECTIONS:

- Exit at **bus stop 2995**, *Hwy 224 & McPolin Farm*. Follow a path towards the barn. Alternatively, exit at **bus stop 3000**, *Hwy 224 Outbound* and find a path to the underpass and follow directions for drivers.

- **Drivers** may find parking at the trailhead east of Route 224, across the highway from the white barn. Turn north out of the parking area. Follow the paved path to a fork and bear left (west) to go through an underpass. Bear right coming out of the underpass.

- Turn left on one of the paved paths into the farm property.

- Follow paved paths around the buildings where plaques provide historical information. Find another paved path behind the buildings, the **Farm Trail**.

- Turn left, heading south. The path crosses Meadows Drive, Payday Drive, and Prospector Drive. The next corner is a four-way intersection at Thaynes Canyon Drive with pushbutton crosswalks. Cross Route 224. Once across the highway, find a sidewalk to the left of Snow Creek Drive. It crosses roads, bends into the Snow Creek Shopping Center and turns left into a parking lot. Follow it to find another paved path to the left, opposite the southwest corner of the parking lot.

- Turn left onto this path, the **McLeod Creek Trail**. It crosses Saddle View Way and then turns right and left. There are two more road crossings before return to **parking** on the east side of Route 224, or bus stops along 224.

ROUTE SUMMARY:

o   From the bus stop or trailhead along Route 224, find paved paths into and through the McPolin Farm property. Find the paved Farm Trail behind the buildings.

o   Turn left and proceed south. Cross three streets and come to a four-way intersection at the corner of Thaynes Canyon Drive.

o   Cross Route 224. Find a sidewalk along the left side of Snow Creek Drive. Follow it into the shopping center parking to find a paved path to the left.

o   Turn left onto this path and follow it through some turns and street crossings back to start.

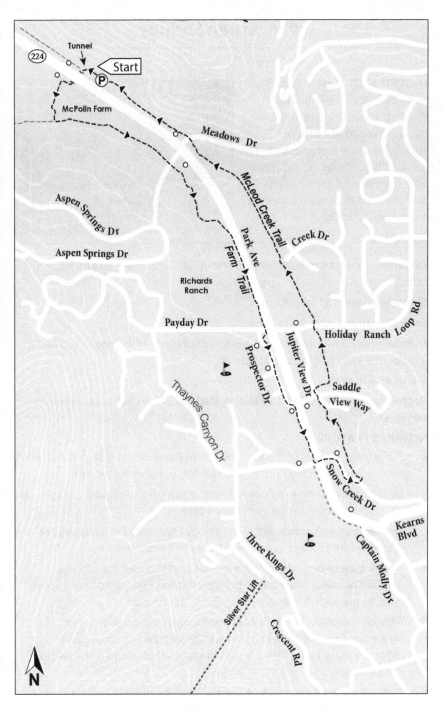

#15 Farm Trail – McLeod Creek Trail

#16 Aspen Springs

DESCRIPTION: West of Park City's entry corridor, this walk winds through a serene alpine neighborhood set amidst aspens, spring fed water features, and luscious landscapes. It's approachable from several access points and provides maximal exercise for a quick, quiet walk.

Distance: about 2.5 miles (4 km) for drivers, about 2 miles (3.2 km) for bus riders.

Elevation Gain: 285 feet (87 m)

Peak Elevation: 7,035 feet (21 m)

Difficulty: INTERMEDIATE due to a long uphill climb at the beginning and a long gentle ascent at the end for drivers.

Surface: All paved.

Restrooms may be available in **Rotary Park** for drivers but are a detour for bus riders.

NOTABLE FEATURES:

◊   Enjoy unique views of the iconic **McPolin Farm**. When foliage is not in full array, you can catch glimpses of magnificent mountain estates.

◊   **Horses** graze summer pastures. Because this neighborhood snuggles up against the mountain, be alert for **wildlife**.

◊   The **springs** and **ponds** in Aspen Springs are created when gravity or pressure causes water in aquifers to flow to Earth's surface.

◊   A **rock quarry** projects from the mountainside above the highest perched homes. Lonely outcroppings of rocks signal tectonically active areas to geologists and miners.

◊   A metal sculpture, symbolic of **Olympic rings**, captures views of ski terrain. Deer Valley Resort hosted Olympic slalom, aerials, and moguls events. Park City Mountain hosted half-pipe and giant slalom competitions.

◊   **Richards Ranch**, just north of Payday Drive, provides 20-acres of protected open space, as described in Walk #15.

◊ At the west end of Payday Drive, where miners once picked up paychecks, find **Rotary Park**, a municipal facility that citizens can rent for private parties.

◊ For drivers in need of some butt-busting exercise, take a **detour** up Iron Canyon Drive instead of turning right on Delta Drive. Then turn right onto Iron Mountain Drive, loop back to Iron Canyon Drive and turn left at the 4-way intersection onto Delta Drive to walk the loop described below. Bus riders can also take this detour by turning south onto Delta Drive.

DIRECTIONS:

■ **Bus stop 2585**, *Park Ave & Meadows Dr to Park City*, puts you on Meadows Drive. **Bus stop 2590**, *Park Ave & Meadows Dr Outbound*, gets you to start if you carefully cross the Highway. Proceed west on Meadows Drive to a T-intersection.

■ Turn left onto Aspen Springs Drive and loop back to Meadows Drive and you're back to the bus stops.

■ **Drivers** should turn west off of Route 224 onto Payday Drive and proceed to Rotary Park and limited parking at the end of the street on the right.

■ Walk east on Payday, and immediately turn left onto Iron Canyon Drive. Continue uphill to an intersection with Delta Drive.

■ Turn right onto Delta, a short street.

■ From Delta Drive turn left onto Aspen Springs Drive, and follow it up, around and down a big horseshoe. After passing a ranch behind the white barn, turn left onto Meadows Drive and follow it to Route 224.

■ Turn right onto a paved trail just before the highway, the **Farm Trail**. Follow it past the Olympic Rings trailhead to the intersection at Payday Drive.

■ Turn right onto Payday. Your vehicle is at the end of this street.

ROUTE SUMMARY:

o Bus riders ascend Meadows Drive, on the west side of Rt. 224. Turn left onto Aspens Springs Drive and follow it around and back to Meadows Drive for the bus.

o Drivers should walk east from Rotary Park at the west end of Payday Drive and turn left onto Iron Canyon Drive.

o Turn right onto Delta Drive.

o Turn left onto Aspen Springs Drive and follow it to a T-intersection.

- o   Turn left onto Meadows Drive and follow it to a paved path just before Route 224.
- o   Turn right onto the paved path and follow to the corner of Payday Drive.
- o   Turn right on Payday and return to the end of the street where you parked.

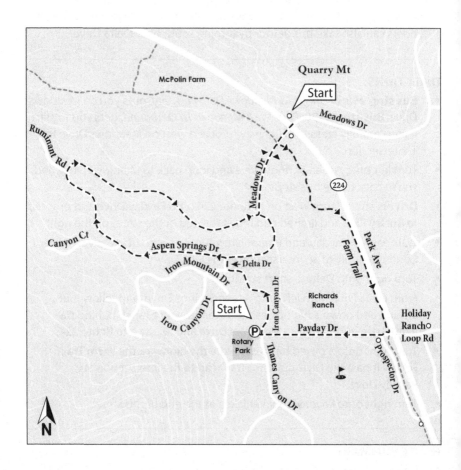

#16 Aspen Springs

#17 Park Meadows

DESCRIPTION: This suburban neighborhood, once occupied by ranches,
now features residences, schools, a
country club golf course and public
recreation options.

Distance: 4.9 miles (7.9 km)

Elevation Gain: 131 feet (40 m)

Peak Elevation: 6,693 feet (2040 m)

Difficulty: INTERMEDIATE due to its length. Inclines are gentle but there's a
mild ascent at the end.

Surface: All paved.

Restrooms are available in Creekside Park. Another option is a **detour** to the
MARC or school ball field facility as described in Walk #11.

NOTABLE FEATURES:

◊ **Creekside Park** offers a **playground** with agility features, and a **jump
bike park**, as pictured above.

◊ Park Meadows provides **trail connections** to Quarry Mountain, PC Hill,
Round Valley and McLeod Creek. And, when it's getting dark and chilly in
the shadow of the mountain on Park City's west side, Park Meadows is still
sunny and warm.

◊ The **Municipal Athletic and Recreation Center** (the **MARC**) offers gyms,
pools, courts, and classes for residents and visitors.

DIRECTIONS:

▪ Start at **bus stop 20140**, *Holiday Ranch Loop Rd & Creek Dr* across the
street from Creekside Park. **Drivers** can turn east off of Rt. 224 onto
Holiday Ranch Loop. Take the second right hand turn into Creekside Park.

▪ Exiting Creekside Park, turn right onto a paved path along Holiday Ranch
Loop Road. Follow it to an intersection with Little Kate Road.

▪ Turn right onto Little Kate and proceed a short way to an intersection
with Lucky John Drive. (If you briefly continue straight on Little Kate, you
can **detour** to the **MARC**.)

- Turn right onto Lucky John. Follow it past schoolyards and it becomes Meadows Drive. Continue on Meadows to an intersection with Fairway Village Drive.

- Turn left onto Fairway Village. Proceed uphill to an intersection with Sunny Slopes Drive.

- Turn left on Sunny Slopes and proceed downhill and around a bend. Continue on the private road, (private roads are open to the walking public unless the sign says "No Pedestrians" or "Keep Out"). The road bends right and ascends back to Meadows Drive.

- Turn left onto Meadows. Pass the entrance into the country club parking and come to an intersection with American Saddler Drive.

- Turn left and proceed on American Saddler passing multiple left turns. Arrive at a 4-way intersection with Lucky John Drive.

- Turn left onto Lucky John and proceed to Little Kate Road.

- Turn right onto Little Kate and proceed to the intersection with Holiday Ranch Loop Road.

- Turn left onto the path along Holiday Ranch and follow it back to the Creekside Park **bus** stop and **parking**.

ROUTE SUMMARY:
o   Start at Creekside Park on Holiday Ranch Road.
o   From the park, turn right onto Holiday Ranch.
o   Turn right onto Little Kate Road.
o   Turn right onto Lucky John Drive. It becomes Meadows Drive.
o   Turn left onto Fairway Village Drive.
o   Turn left onto Sunny Slopes Drive. Follow it around bends and back up to Meadows Drive.
o   Turn left onto Meadows.
o   Turn left onto American Saddler Drive.
o   Turn left onto Lucky John Drive.
o   Turn right onto Little Kate Road.
o   Turn left onto the Holiday Ranch Loop path to return to start.

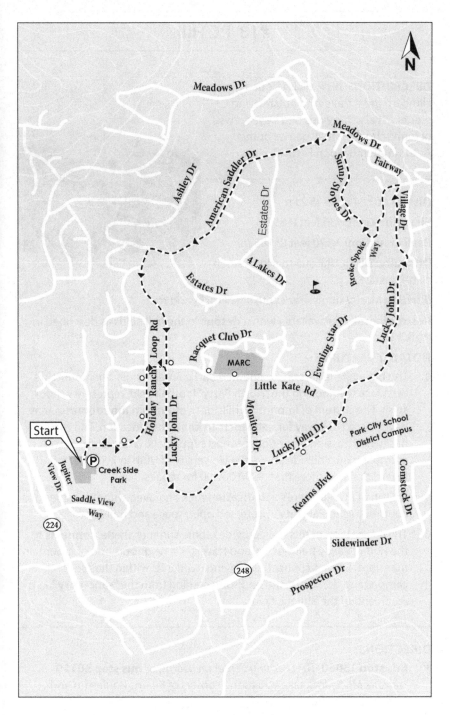

#17 Park Meadows

#18 PC Hill

DESCRIPTION: This walk is about a good climb on great trails with outstanding scenery. It also provides bird's eye views of high school football games or the Autumn Aloft Balloon Festival.

Distance: 3.24 miles (5.2 km)

Elevation Gain: 536 feet (163 m)

Peak Elevation: 7,170 feet (2,185 m)

Difficulty: DIFFICULT due to a long steep climb to start.

Surface: Mostly single-track with small rocks and roots.

Restrooms may be available with a **detour** to the ball fields as described in Walk #11.

NOTABLE FEATURES:

◊   The big white letters "PC" cemented and painted across the mountain's west face overlooking the "North Forty" football field, represent school spirit. The custom of imprinting hillsides, (**mountain monograms**), may have started as a way for railroaders to know their location. The custom has fueled passionate opponents and supporters. When a big "U" was crumbling on a hillside above the University of Utah in 2006, "letter lovers" donated more than $200,000.00 for repairs.

◊   On top of PC Hill, there's a **dedication** rock engraved with the names of contributors to Park City's protected open space and trails.

◊   The return loop of this walk provides some summer shade, **connects** to the Round Valley trail system, and traverses a neighborhood of mountain mansions. Enjoy a connecting trail into wetlands within the school campus and don't miss the bird song coming from the **"sanctuary"** at the south end of the athletic field.

DIRECTIONS:

▪   **Bus stop 15060**, *The Learning Center on Kearns*, or **bus stop 50110**, *Treasure Mt. Kearns*, take you to the corners of Kearns Boulevard and Comstock Avenue.

- **Bus** riders and **drivers** should turn north off of Route 248, Kearns Boulevard, just east of the school campus buildings and just west of PC Hill. Follow this narrow road to a trailhead.

- Find the **PC Hill Trail** opposite a footbridge. Turn right onto this trail to begin the climb. Ascend through a switchback and come to a fork.

- Bear right, switching back again. Continue uphill and southward. Ignore two "fooler" trails to the left and one to the right and arrive at another fork.

- Bear left. The trail then bends east. Stay on the path that appears most used and notice a left turn as a fence comes into view. There's a trail to the left before the fence, and another trail along the fence.

- Turn left onto either trail and proceed through the next left turn onto a trail that bends west and takes you to the "PC" letters. There are uphill trails after the big "P" and "C."

- Take either trail to the mountaintop where there are more trails, including **PC Hill Trail** to the east (opposite the "PC").

- Take PC Hill Trail through switchbacks down the mountain. Cross a double-track road and stay on the single-track. Come to a fork with a sign for the **Quinn Recreation Trail**.

- Bear left. You'll quickly come to a trail intersection with the **Hat Trick Trail**.

- Turn left onto Hat Trick and continue to the next intersection with the **Fairway Hills Connector Trail**.

- Turn left onto Fairway Hills Connector. It ends in the cul-de-sac of Morning Sky Court. Continue downhill on Morning Sky to Silver Cloud Drive.

- Turn left onto Silver Cloud and follow it downhill to Meadows Drive.

- Turn left onto Meadows Drive and walk in the bike lane. Just past a private drive on the left, (that looks like a road), find a blacktop path that goes back to the school fields, and a sign pointing to the **Rail Trail.**

- Turn left onto this path and bear right onto a woodchip trail bordering a fence that goes around the school field. This trail takes you past the "sanctuary" on the south end of the field. On the east side of the field find a footbridge over a creek crossing back to the **parking** at the base of PC Hill.

- From the trailhead, exit south to Kearns Boulevard to get to one of the **bus** stops.

ROUTE SUMMARY:

o   Start at the PC Trailhead at the east end of the school campus and west of PC Hill.

o   Turn right onto the PC Hill Trail. Proceed through two switchbacks, bearing right at an intersection. Ignore "fooler" trails and come to a fork.

o   Bear left. Stay on the trail that appears most used. Notice two left turns as a fence comes into view. Take either. They both turn left and bend west to arrive at the "PC."

o   Take either of the trails that start above the big "P" or "C" to the mountain top.

o   Take the PC Hill Trail down. At an intersection with double-track, cross the road to stay on the single-track. Arrive at a fork with a sign to the Quinn Recreation Trail.

o   Bear left and quickly arrive at the Hat Trick Trail.

o   Turn left onto Hat Trick and come to an intersection.

o   Turn left onto Fairway Hills Connector Trail and proceed to Morning Sky Court. Walk downhill to Silver Cloud Drive.

o   Turn left on Silver Cloud and come to an intersection with Meadows Drive.

o   Turn left on Meadows and continue past a private drive to a blacktop path on the left.

o   Turn left onto this blacktop.

o   Bear right onto a woodchip path encircling the athletic field to arrive at a footbridge that returns to start.

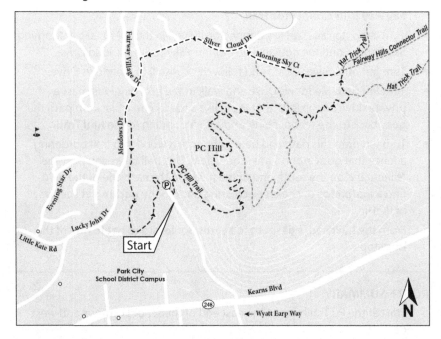

#18 PC Hill

#19 The Cove – Quarry Mountain

DESCRIPTION: This short off-road walk above the Park Meadows neighborhood takes you through surprisingly diverse landscapes on well-maintained trails.

Distance: 1.3 miles (2.0 km)

Elevation Gain: 125 feet (38 m)

Peak Elevation: 6,931 feet (1,871 m)

Difficulty: INTERMEDIATE due to a mild but steady climb at the start.

Surface: Dirt paths, sidewalk and some rocky terrain.

Restrooms are not available.

NOTABLE FEATURES:

◊ In 2014, Park City Municipal procured 53 acres on Risner Ridge as protected **open space**. This land serves as a view shed and supports elk, moose, mule deer, foxes, rabbits, squirrels, raptors, and other wildlife, as well as walkers, equestrians, and snowshoers.

◊ Some of this route feels like remote country. You will briefly traverse a **rock quarry**.

◊ **Trailhead bulletin boards** as pictured here, can provide important safety information.

◊ There are other trails and quarries on **Quarry Mountain**, (and a cell phone tower). This route can easily be **combined** with Walk #20 Lah Dee Duh. They share a starting point.

DIRECTIONS:

- Expect a 1 1/4-mile (2 km) uphill walk to the trailhead from **bus stop 20060**, *Little Kate Rd & Evening Star Dr.* Proceed east on Little Kate to an intersection with Lucky John Drive.

- Turn left onto Lucky John. It becomes Meadows Drive. After a second climb and a big left bend, find the Cove Trailhead on the right. (Bus riders could take the drivers' route, but it's a long steep climb.)

- **Drivers** turn east off of Route 224 at Meadows Drive. Proceed up a long hill about 1 1/2 miles (2.4 km) and find a trailhead and parking on the left before the road bends right.

- Find a dirt trail, the **Rossman Trail**, across the street from the Cove Trailhead. Bear right onto this trail. Ignore turnoffs and arrive at a road.
- Cross the road to pick up the trail on the opposite side. It winds around a flat boulder and quickly intersects with gravel double-track.
- Turn right onto the double-track. Proceed uphill and to the left around a water tank, then downhill to a T-intersection with single-track.
- Turn left onto the single-track. Follow it to arrive at another T-intersection. (To take a short **detour** to a lookout, turn right at the T to arrive at a bench dedicated to the trail's namesake, Norman Rossman, a New York City builder who adored Park City.)
- To skip the lookout, turn left at the T-intersection and it becomes a double-track. (Returning from the lookout, bear right at this intersection.) Proceed to a four-way intersection.
- Turn left onto a gravel road and follow it to Meadows Drive.
- **Drivers** should turn left onto Meadows and proceed back to the trailhead. **Bus** riders can turn right onto Meadows and follow it to the bus stop at its intersection with Route 224, a long walk, but mostly downhill. Or, turn left and follow Meadows Drive to Lucky John to Little Kate and the bus stop.

ROUTE SUMMARY:

o   Start at the Cove Trailhead on Meadows Drive. Cross the street from the trailhead and turn right onto the Rossman Trail. Follow it to a paved road.

o   Cross the road and pick up the same trail between some rocks. Proceed to an intersection.

o   Turn right and ascend on a dirt road to the left side of a water tank and downhill to an intersection with a single-track.

o   **Detour** to a lookout or turn left and proceed to the next trail intersection.

o   Turn left and proceed to another intersection.

o   Turn left onto a gravel road and follow it to Meadows Drive.

o   Turn left onto the sidewalk along Meadows to return to parking at the Cove Trailhead. Bus riders can turn right onto Meadows and walk downhill to a bus stop or turn left to return to start.

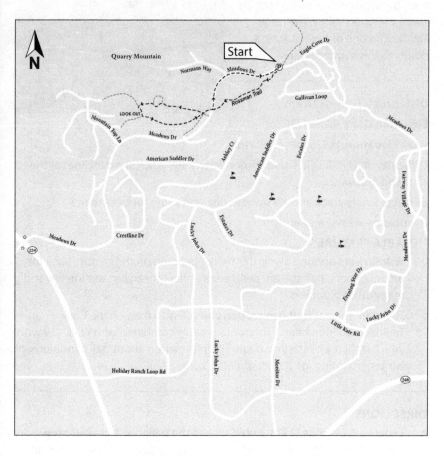

#19 The Cove – Quarry Mountain

#20 Lah Dee Duh

DESCRIPTION: On the east edge of suburban Park City, walkers will find a network of well-maintained trails traversing the preserved open space of Round Valley. The Cove Trailhead is one of several access points to this expansive area.

Distance: 1.3 miles (2.0 km)

Elevation Gain: 92 feet (28 m)

Peak Elevation: 6,875 feet (2,096 m)

Difficulty: INTERMEDIATE due to moderately steep but short inclines at the start and midway.

Surface: Single-track, mostly smooth dirt, and some rocky terrain.

Restrooms are not available.

NOTABLE FEATURES:

◊ **Wildflowers** abound along this trail depending on the season. Look for onion, chicory, paintbrush, penstemon, prickly pear, lily, sunflowers, and many other bloomers.

◊ There are several **trail connections** here. Find a map on the Cove Trailhead bulletin board. This route is easily combined with Walk #19 with which it shares its starting point. For information about trail conditions, or winter grooming, go to *mountaintrails.org*.

DIRECTIONS:

■ Expect a 1 1/4-mile (2 km) uphill walk to the trailhead from **bus stop 20060**, *Little Kate Rd & Evening Star Dr*. Proceed east on Little Kate to an intersection with Lucky John Drive.

■ Turn left onto Lucky John. It becomes Meadows Drive. After a second climb and a big left bend, find the Cove Trailhead on the right. (Bus riders could take the drivers' route, but it's a long steep climb.)

■ **Drivers** turn east off of Route 224 at Meadows Drive. Proceed up a long hill about 1 1/2 Miles (2.4 km) and look for a trailhead and parking on the left before the road bends right.

- From the Cove Trailhead, follow the rocky dirt road uphill. Bear right at the first fork, left at the second fork, and left at the third fork onto a single-track, **Lah Dee Duh Trail**. Proceed until you notice an unmarked trail to the left, shortly before seeing a sign for **Cammy's Trail** on the right.
- Turn left onto this unmarked downhill single-track. Go about a tenth of a mile (0.17 km) and find another single-track trail to the right.
- Turn right and briefly climb rock steps for another tenth of a mile (0.17 km) to reconnect with Lah Dee Duh.
- Turn right onto Lah Dee Duh and follow it back to the trailhead and **parking**, taking right turns at intersections. **Bus** riders can turn right onto Meadows and follow it to the bus stop at its intersection with Route 224, a long walk, but mostly downhill. Or, turn left and walk on Meadows Drive to Lucky John Drive to Little Kate Road and the bus stop.

ROUTE SUMMARY:
o From the Cove Trailhead, head east uphill and come to three forks.
o Bear right at the first fork, left at the second, and left at the third fork.
o Follow this single-track to an unmarked trail on the left.
o Turn left. Proceed downhill to an unmarked trail on the right.
o Turn right and climb some rock steps back to a single-track.
o Turn right and follow the trail back to start, bearing right at intersections.

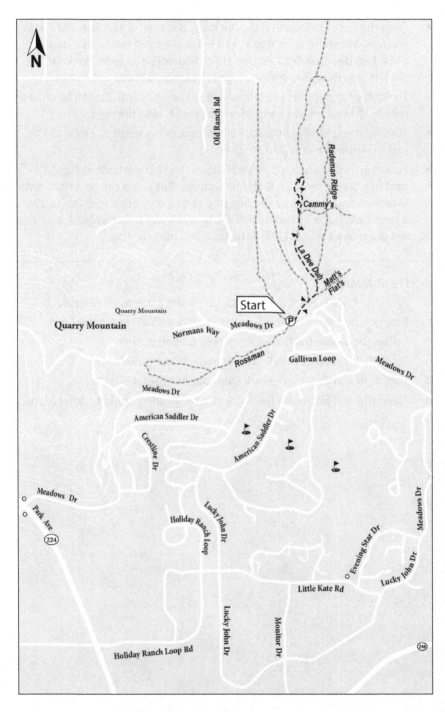

#20 Lah Dee Duh

#21 Fairway Hills

DESCRIPTION: A "gold mine" of groomed trails traverses open space between the Park Meadows neighborhood and Quinn's Junction. This route takes you past lush farmland and exquisite residences.

Distance: 1.8 miles (2.9 km)

Elevation Gain: 125 feet (38 m)

Peak Elevation: 6,930 feet (2,112 m)

Difficulty: EASY, elevation gain is well-distributed.

Surface: Mostly roadbed on single and double-track.

Restrooms are not available.

NOTABLE FEATURES:

◊ This walk is an interesting blend of gentrified and native. Check the trailhead bulletin board regarding potential **wildlife** encounters.

◊ Find **maps** and information on the bulletin board. Before attempting to navigate the complex trail system here, check *mountaintrails.org* or consult *Park City Hiking Guide*, (available in local stores and at major online booksellers), for maps and directions through Round Valley from five different access points.

DIRECTIONS:

- Expect a 1 1/4-mile (2 km) uphill walk to the trailhead from **bus stop 20060**, *Little Kate Rd & Evening Star Dr*. Proceed east on Little Kate to an intersection with Lucky John Drive. Lucky John becomes Meadows Drive. Continue to Sunny Slopes Drive, a right turn.

- **Drivers** turn east off of Route 224 at Meadows Drive. Follow it to the east end of the neighborhood. Sunny Slopes Drive will be a left turn.

- Proceed uphill on Sunny Slopes to the second left turn, Fairway Hills Court.

- Turn left onto Fairway Hills and immediately turn right onto Round Valley Way, a cul-de-sac with a trailhead. Beware the big bump at the parking entrance.

- Check trailhead notices. Proceed through the parking area and turn right onto the **Fast Pitch Trail**. Proceed on this single-track about 1/3 mile (0.53 km) to the first right turn.
- Turn right onto the **Hat Trick Trail** and proceed about a 1/2 mile (0.8 km) until you come to an intersecting trail, **Fairway Hills Connector.**
- Turn right onto the Connector and follow this trail until it ends on a cul-de-sac. Descend on the sidewalk to Silver Cloud Drive.
- Cross Silver Cloud. Find a double-track trail behind a fire hydrant. Follow this trail to Sunny Slopes Drive, ignoring forks along the way.
- Cross Sunny Slopes, turn left, and descend to a four-way intersection with Fairway Hills Court.
- If you came by **bus**, continue down Sunny Slopes to Meadows Drive. Turn left on Meadows and follow it to Little Kate Road.
- Turn right and proceed to the bus stop on Little Kate.
- **Drivers** should turn right onto Fairway Hills Court and immediately turn right again onto Round Valley Way.
- From parking, turn left and then right to descend to Meadows Drive.
- Turn right onto Meadows to get to Route 224.

ROUTE SUMMARY:

o   Start at the Round Valley Trailhead in the east end of Park Meadows.

o   Turn right out of the parking area onto the Fast Pitch Trail and come to an intersection.

o   Turn right onto Hat Trick Trail. Proceed to an intersection and turn right onto the Fairway Hills Connector Trail, which ends on Morning Sky Court.

o   Descend the road to Silver Cloud Drive, cross the street and find a double-track trail behind a fire hydrant. Proceed on this trail until it ends on Sunny Slopes Drive.

o   Cross Sunny Slopes to the sidewalk and turn left. Descend to a four-way intersection.

o   Bus riders continue down Sunny Slopes and turn left onto Meadows Drive.

o   Drivers turn right onto Fairway Hills Court and make another quick right onto Round Valley Way to return to parking.

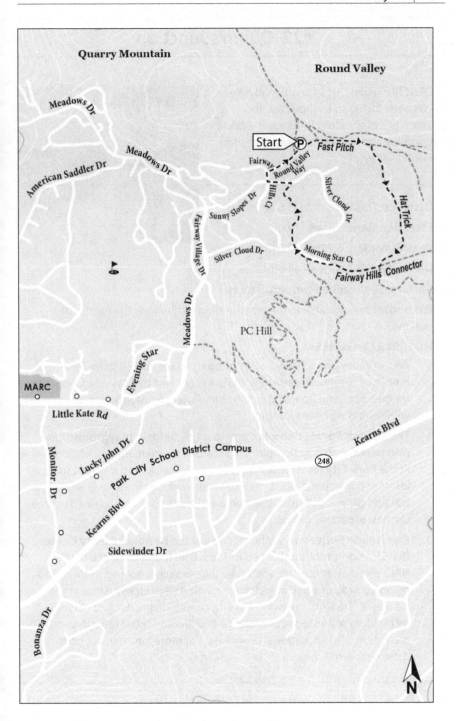

#21 Fairway Hills

#22 Quinn's Junction

DESCRIPTION: This easy off-road hike has been included to showcase the amenities of the Quinn's Junction Sports Complex and some of the easier trails in Round Valley.

Distance: This is a 1-mile (1.6 km) loop

Elevation Gain: 62 feet (19 m)

Peak Elevation: 6,718 ft. (2,048 m)

Difficulty: EASY, though all off-road.

Surface: Dirt roadbed with small rocks.

Restrooms are available in the freestanding facility near the ball fields parking.

NOTABLE FEATURES:

◊ Round Valley provides 690 acres of **open space** and 30 miles (48km) of trails, but barely comprises 7% of Park City's vast trail system. Check the trailhead bulletin board or *mountaintrails.org* for information about trails, wildlife and winter grooming.

◊ The **Quinn's Sports Complex** provides ball **fields**, a **playground**, and **dog parks**. Watch a championship softball tournament or a hockey game at the **Park City Ice Arena**. After your walk, ice-skating on a hot summer afternoon is a cool delight. Your summer walking clothes will work if you just add gloves, but small children are closer to the ice and need warmer clothes, especially gloves.

◊ Pass by lush farmland and the facilities of the **National Ability Center (NAC)**, a non-profit established in 1985. Due to the presence of the NAC, you may encounter adaptive athletes skiing, golfing, cycling, and on horseback, or you can watch an exciting sled hockey game at the ice arena. The NAC's mission is to empower individuals of all abilities by building self-esteem, confidence and lifetime skills through sport, recreation, and educational programs. For more information, go to *www.discovernac.org*.

DIRECTIONS (ROUTE SUMMARY):

- **Bus** service to Quinn's Junction may be available from the Kamas Commuter bus line or bus riders may arrange for free shared service by calling 435.640.7819.

- **Drivers** turn west off of Route 248 onto Round Valley Drive at the traffic light west of Route 40. Take the first left turn onto Gillmor Way. Park in the second parking area near the ball fields.

- Find the Quinn's Trailhead bulletin board across the road from the ballfield parking where three trails converge. Take the middle trail, **Fast Pitch** and proceed to an intersection.

- Turn right onto the **Hat Trick Trail** and follow it back to the trailhead to return to start.

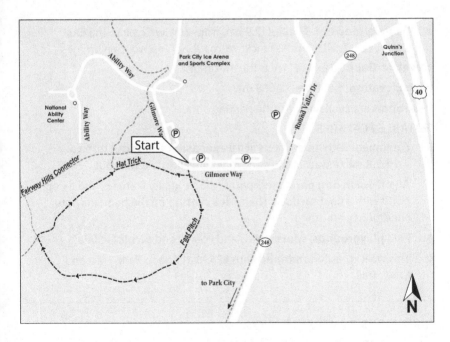

#22 Quinn's Junction

#23 Willow Creek Park

DESCRIPTION: Multiple walks and amenities are available in this 17.5-acre community park adjoined by 66 acres of open space.

Distance, Surface, and Difficulty for three walks: These are all EASY short walks on level trails that may be groomed in winter.

o   The shortest walk is 0.33 miles (0.5 km), all blacktop.

o   A 1-mile (1.6-km) loop along the **Willow Creek** and **Split Rail Trails** includes level blacktop and roadbed.

o   A longer loop of 1.83 miles (2.9 km) from Willow Creek to the **East Connector Trail** includes blacktop, roadbed, and wooden bridges.

Elevation Gain: 70 feet (21 m) is the maximum

Peak Elevation: 6,558 feet (2,008 m)

Restrooms are available near the parking area.

NOTABLE FEATURES:

◊   Equipment with instructions at **10 exercise stations** can turn your workout into a walk in the park, or your walk into a workout.

◊   An **off-leash dog park** offers paths, shade, agility features, and a dog pond with a floating dock. There's **ice skating** on the pond in winter, conditions permitting.

◊   Find **playgrounds**, **sports** fields and courts, and **picnic** facilities.

◊   This walk is easily **combined** with #24 Matt Knoop Park – McLeod Creek Trail.

DIRECTIONS(ROUTE SUMMARY):

▪   **Bus stop 4280**, *Hwy 224 & Old Ranch Rd* is just north of Old Ranch Road. **Drivers** take Route 224 to Old Ranch Road and turn east.

▪   Take the sidewalk or drive along Old Ranch, which bends left and then right. Find Willowcreek Park and parking on your left in about 0.65 miles (1.05 km).

▪   Maps and signs within the park provide directions and bring you back to start.

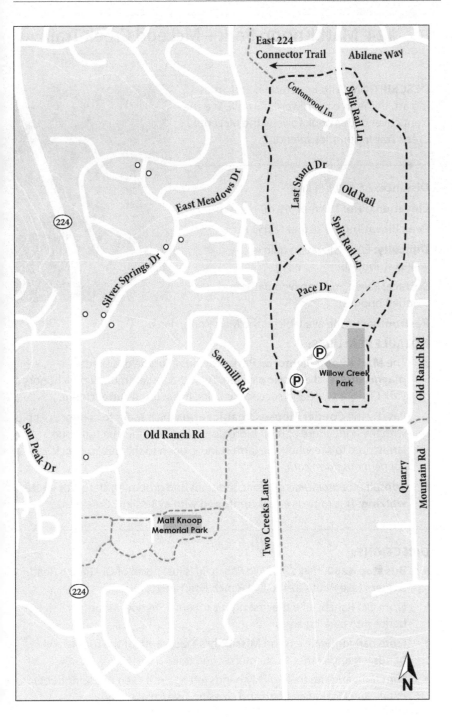

#23 Willow Creek Park

#24 Matt Knoop Park – McLeod Creek Trail

DESCRIPTION: With level terrain and amusing art, this is an easy, rewarding walk. See the front cover of this book to view the McLeod Creek Trail in summer splendor.

Distance: 2.5 miles (4 km)

Elevation Gain: 161 feet (49 m)

Peak Elevation: 6,728 feet (2,051 m)

Difficulty: EASY, elevation gain is well-distributed.

Surface: Paved and unpaved paths and wooden bridges.

Restrooms may be available at the Matt Knoop Park.

NOTABLE FEATURES:

◊ The **Matt Knoop Memorial Park** provides a turf field, a shaded **playground**, and a **picnic** pavilion. This 10-acre community park honors a Park City graduate and soccer star killed in a hit-and-run accident.

◊ Pass by the **Copper Moose Organic Farm** which seeks to connect people with the agriculture of their bioregion and makes for a picturesque landscape. To see when the farm stand is open to the public, check *coppermoosefarm.com*.

◊ Consult *mountaintrails.org* for conditions and grooming status for **winter walking**. This route is easily **combined** with #23 Willow Creek Park.

DIRECTIONS:

▪ **Bus stop 4280**, *Hwy 224 & Old Ranch Rd* is just north of Old Ranch Road. **Drivers** take Route 224 to Old Ranch Road and turn east.

▪ From Old Ranch, take the first right turn onto Shadow Mountain Drive. It bends into parking areas.

▪ From parking, walk east on **Miss Billy's Trail**, south of the turf field. It bends left and comes to an intersecting trail.

▪ Turn right and the trail quickly bends left again. It then bends right before paralleling Old Ranch Road and crossing Two Creeks Lane.

- Quickly turn right onto roadbed after crossing Two Creeks and continue on the **McLeod Creek Trail** as it makes two 90-degree turns and crosses a boardwalk. Look for sculpted metal flowers. Pass between them and follow a footpath through a wooded area to a fork.
- Bear left at the fork and follow the path around Temple Har Shalom.
- Turn left onto a road into the temple parking lot and follow it west to Route 224. Find a pedestrian path alongside the highway.
- Turn right heading north on this path where there are **bus** stops. **Drivers** pass two intersections. Come to a gravel road on the right, Miss Billy's Bypass and Ike's Pump Track.
- Turn right off the paved path towards Miss Billy's. Come to a fork.
- Bear right to return to Matt Knoop Park parking.

ROUTE SUMMARY:

o   Start at the parking area of Matt Knoop Memorial Park.

o   Take Miss Billy's Trail south of the turf field to a trail intersection.

o   Turn right and follow this trail through bends and a road intersection, Two Creeks Lane.

o   Cross Two Creeks and immediately turn right onto roadbed. Follow it over a wooden bridge to find metal flowers. Pass between the flowers. Proceed to a fork.

o   Bear left. Proceed around Temple Har Shalom and parking. Continue to Route 224.

o   Turn right onto a paved path alongside the highway. Walking north, pass two intersections and come to Miss Billy's Bypass Trail on your right. Turn right onto Miss Billy's and bear right at a fork to return to parking.

o   Bus riders will have optional stops along Route 224.

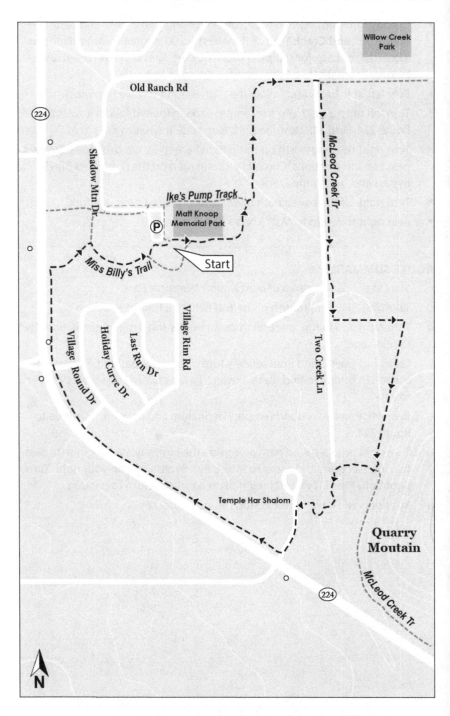

#24 Matt Knoop Park – McLeod Creek Trail

#25 Swaner Preserve – Redstone

DESCRIPTION: This short, easy walk takes you on a neighborhood trail around the periphery of a nature preserve and through a commercial plaza.

Distance: 1.5 miles (2.4 km)

Elevation Gain: 33 feet (10 m)

Peak Elevation: 6,428 feet (1,959 m)

Difficulty: EASY, relatively level.

Surface: Paved trails and sidewalks.

Restrooms may be found at various businesses in the commercial area.

NOTABLE FEATURES:

◊ **Swaner Memorial Park** ("The Preserve") was created by the Swaner Family in 1995 along with the land trust, Utah Open Lands. Conservation easements here protect wildlife within 1,200 acres of **open space** and 800 acres of wetlands. There are 10 miles (16 km) of trails and a historic farm within the preserve.

◊ **The Swaner Ecocenter**, 1258 Center Drive, (*swanerecocenter.org*), is an ecology museum with changing exhibits, an observation tower, guided tours, geocaching adventures (treasure hunts using GPS devices), a gift shop, and snowshoe rentals for winter walks.

◊ The **obelisk** in the Newpark Town Center casts a shadow on the pavement showing the sun's motion through the calendar year.

◊ **Dining** and **shopping** opportunities are plentiful here.

DIRECTIONS (ROUTE SUMMARY):

▪ **Exit bus stop 78050**, *Newpark Hotel on Highland Dr.* Walk south and turn left (east) around the hotel onto Newpark Boulevard and walk to a plaza at the end of the street.

▪ **Drivers** turn east from Rt. 224 at Kimball Junction onto Newpark Boulevard. Go 180 degrees around the traffic circle and continue east. Cross Highland Drive and Newpark ends at a plaza. Parking may be available at nearby lots or a parking garage.

- The Ecocenter is in the northeast corner of the plaza. A paved path starts at the southwest corner of the Ecocenter. Bear left from the plaza onto this path and follow it as it encircles townhomes.
- Bear right when the path intersects with the trail bordering Route. 224.
- At the next trail intersection; turn right onto Redstone Center Drive, crossing under the arched sign. Proceed to a road intersection.
- Cross Highland Drive at the intersection and continue onto New Main Street, veering left back to the plaza, **bus** stops and **parking**.

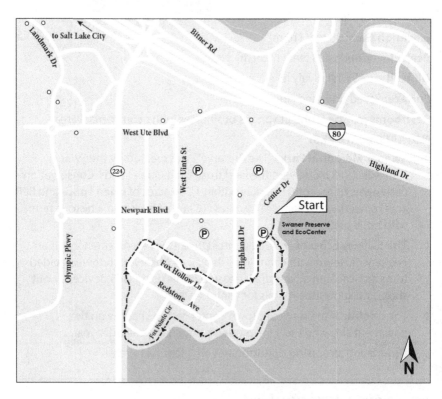

#25 Swaner Preserve – Redstone

#26 Over and Under Kimball Junction

DESCRIPTION: Enjoy this route up, over, down, and under roads and retail, while those in your group who'd rather hunt for designer deals can shop Outlets Park City.

Distance: 2.8 miles (4.5 km)

Elevation Gain: 148 feet (45m)

Peak Elevation: 6,496 feet (1980 m)

Difficulty: EASY, though with some gentle inclines.

Surface: Sidewalk, blacktop, and minimal dirt footpath.

Restrooms are available at the Outlets and Visitor's Center.

NOTABLE FEATURES:

◊   An **overpass** takes walkers above the Interstate highway, while clever conversion of a culvert provides an **underpass**.

◊   The **Snyderville Basin Field House** provides **playgrounds**, indoor golf and batting cages, a track, climbing walls, exercise equipment, and classes, *basinrecreation.org*.

◊   See Walk #25 for information about the **Swaner Preserve Ecocenter**. Additional trails are available from the **Spring Creek Trailhead**, a **detour** from this route.

◊   **Dining** and **shopping** options are plentiful.

DIRECTIONS:

■   Exit at **bus stop 70090**, *Outlets Park City* or **park** near The Outlets "moose" entrance on Landmark Drive.

■   Find a paved path behind the stores on the southeast end of the mall.

■   Turn right onto this path and follow it as it bends left and arrives at an elevated bridge over Route 80. Proceed from the bridge straight onto a sidewalk that borders Rasmussen Road. Continue southeast along this frontage road and pass three intersections. The third one is Glenwild Drive. (A left turn onto Glenwild enables a **detour** to the Spring Creek Trailhead with a map and access to additional trails through the nature preserve.)

- Cross Glenwild Drive and turn right to carefully cross Rasmussen Road. Immediately to the left, find a footpath to an underpass. Exit the tunnel near the Basin Recreation (Snyderville) Field House.

- Bear left around the field house and find a sign for the **224-Connector Trail**. Follow it as it briefly borders the Swaner Nature Preserve and then intersects with the Newpark Town Plaza (see Walk #25).

- Cross the plaza to Newpark Boulevard. Walk west on Newpark and shortly before it ends, find a paved path to the left, bordering West Redstone Avenue.

- Turn left onto this path and turn right at an intersecting paved path that takes you to a tunnel under Route 224. Continue straight out of the tunnel onto a paved path that ends at the Olympic Parkway.

- Cross Olympic Parkway and turn right, following around a traffic circle to a sidewalk west of Landmark Drive. Pass more commercial areas and the sidewalk delivers you back to The Outlets **bus** stop and **parking**. Bus stop options on the way back can reduce walking.

ROUTE SUMMARY:

o   Start on a paved trail behind the stores at the southeast end of The Outlets mall. Follow it over the highway and continue straight on a trail along Rasmussen Road.

o   Cross Glenwild Drive and immediately cross Rasmussen Road. Find a footpath to the left.

o   Follow the footpath under the highway. Bear left out of the tunnel.

o   Take the 224-Connector Trail a short way to the Newpark Town Plaza. Cross the plaza to Newpark Boulevard and proceed to near its end where there's a paved path to the left.

o   Turn left on this path and turn right at the next path to arrive at a tunnel.

o   Cross under Route 224 and proceed straight until this path ends at Olympic Parkway.

o   Cross the Olympic Parkway and turn right onto sidewalk that follows around a traffic circle and along Landmark Drive back to The Outlets mall.

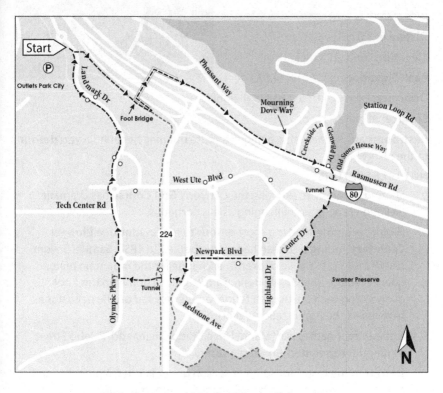

#26 Over and Under Kimball Junction

#27 The Canyons – Sun Peak

DESCRIPTION: This walk takes you past the Canyons Golf Course, and the adjoining Sun Peak neighborhood with its enviable scenery, trails, and properties.

Distance: 3.0 miles (4.8 km)

Elevation Gain: 272 feet (83 m)

Peak Elevation: 6,804 feet (2,073 m)

Difficulty: DIFFICULT. First half is all uphill.

Surface: All paved roads.

Restrooms are not available along this route but may be found if you **detour** to the resort base.

NOTABLE FEATURES:

◊ Sharing terrain with ski trails, the **Canyons Golf Course** has dramatic elevations and is as challenging as it is gorgeous.

◊ Highly recommended is a short **detour** to the **Snyderville Pioneer Cemetery**, hiding between handsome homes. In 1850, Samuel Snyder paid Parley Pratt a yoke of oxen in exchange for the mountain plateau now called the Snyderville Basin. Samuel built a home on this knoll overlooking the plateau. The tender ages engraved on the headstones here reveal the homesteaders' hardships.

◊ Notice street names like "Mahre Drive," "Kidd Circle," and "Picabo Street" that honor **renowned American skiers**.

◊ **Detour** to the resort for summer season gondola rides, alpine disc golf, a bike park, zip line tours, horseback riding, mountain lake fishing, pedal boats, mountain biking, hiking, and dining. The **cabriolet** is an **aerial transport** system from parking to the Canyons Village. It's a free ride but operates only during peak times.

DIRECTIONS (ROUTE SUMMARY):

▪ Exit at **bus stop 51**, *Canyons Transit Hub*. **Drivers** turn west off of Rt. 224 onto Canyons Drive. Follow around a traffic circle to parking.

▪ From parking or the bus stop, walk west on Canyons Drive back to the traffic circle.

- Turn right onto Frostwood Drive. Continue to another circle.
- Bear right onto Cooper Lane.
- Turn left onto Sunpeak Drive.
- Turn left onto Bear Hollow Drive and proceed uphill.
- At the third right corner, turn right onto Mahre Drive, a horseshoe.
- To **detour** to the cemetery, take the 4th left turn off of Maher Drive, Roffe Road. Proceed up a short hill to a cul-de-sac. The cemetery is on the left. Upon return to Mahre Drive, turn left and proceed to the intersection with Bear Hollow Drive.
- Turn right onto Bear Hollow Drive.
- Turn left onto Sun Peak Drive.
- Turn right onto Cooper Lane, which ends at a traffic circle.
- Bear left onto Frostwood Drive and proceed to another circle.
- Bear left onto Canyons Drive to return to the **parking** and **bus** stop.

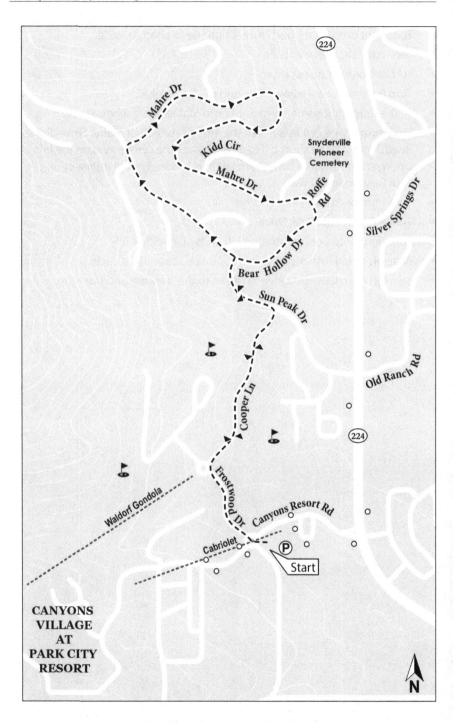

#27 The Canyons – Sun Peak

#28 Bear Hollow – Olympic Park

DESCRIPTION: This challenging route provides awesome views and a tour of the venue that hosted 14 medal competitions in the 2002 winter games. Watching aerialists train by skiing off of ramps and flipping into a pool is the most exhilarating show in town. Make this difficult route easy by taking the free bus from the Visitor Center to the Olympic Park Museums, and another free bus to the
top of the Olympic Park, when available. Then walk back downhill on Olympic Parkway or on Bear Hollow Drive.

Distance: 7 miles (11.3 km), but 4 miles (6.4 km) if you take the buses

Elevation Gain: 892 feet (272 m) if you walk

Peak Elevation: 7,328 feet (2,234 m)

Difficulty: DIFFICULT. This is the most demanding walk in the book due to its length and elevation gain.

Surface: All paved roads with narrow shoulders and switchbacks.

Restrooms may be available in the Visitor's Center and park museums.

NOTABLE FEATURES:

◊   Enjoy **views** of the Canyons Golf Course, Silver Springs Lakes, and the **Uinta Mountains**. The Uintas are the tallest east-west chain of mountains in the U.S.

◊   Woods along the way shelter wildlife. Amicable goats and chickens might greet you at **Bill White Farms** along the paved **Millennial Trail**.

◊   This route borders the bobsled and luge/skeleton tracks in the 387-acre **Olympic Park**, where there are all-season training facilities. Guided tours and lessons are available. Olympic Park also offers trails, bobsled rides, zip lines, adventure courses, an obstacle course, a free chairlift ride at peak times, and shopping. Enjoy **free admission** to the **Alf Engen Ski History Museum** and the **George Eccles 2002 Olympic Winter Games Museum**. Exhibits include virtual chairlift, ramp jumping, and avalanche experiences. If you don't care to do the big Bear Hollow walk, visit the museums anyway, *utaholympiclegacy.org*.

DIRECTIONS:

- Ride to **bus stop 6357**, *Hwy 224 & Olympic Parkway*, or **park** at the Visitor Center on the northwest corner of Route 224 and Newpark Boulevard.

- For the **easy route, inquire in the Park City Visitor Center about free bus service**. If you take a bus to the park top, you can walk the bus route in reverse, or pass through a pedestrian gate onto Bear Hollow Road and follow it downhill to Route 224. Turn left onto the **Millennial Trail** to walk along 224 to return to start.

- If you're doing the big walk starting at the Visitor's Center, cross Newpark Boulevard and proceed south on the Millennial Trail along Rt. 224, about 1.9 miles (3.1 km) to Bear Hollow Drive.

- Turn right onto Bear Hollow and continue west, climbing for approximately 2 miles (3.2 km) to the gate at the top of the Olympic Park. Find a pedestrian entry around the gate and descend along the Olympic Parkway for approximately three miles (4.8 km).

- Upon exiting the park, just before a traffic circle, turn right onto the paved Millennial Trail and proceed east to the Visitor Center, **parking** and the **bus** stop.

ROUTE SUMMARY:

o   Start at the Visitor Center on Rt. 224 and Newpark Boulevard, the Olympic Parkway.

o   Cross Olympic Parkway to find the paved Millennial Trail along Rt. 224. Proceed south to Bear Hollow Drive.

o   Turn right onto Bear Hollow Drive and ascend 2 miles. At the top, find a gate into Olympic Park and descend on the Olympic Parkway to exit the park.

o   Turn right onto the Millennial Trail before a traffic circle to return to start.

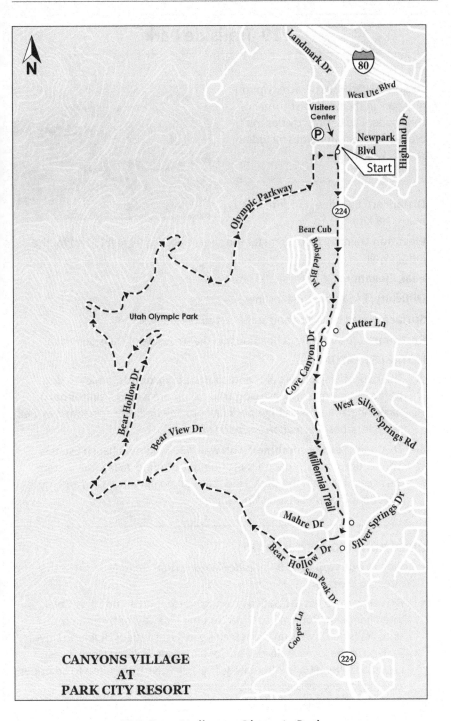

#28 Bear Hollow – Olympic Park

#29 Trailside Park

DESCRIPTION: This 63-acre community park in the northeast corner of the Snyderville Basin provides multiple recreational amenities including several walking routes.

Distance: 0.65 miles (1.05 km) or 1.12 miles (1.8 km)

Elevation Gain: 59 feet (18 m) for the short walk and 98 feet (30 m) for the longer walk

Peak Elevation: 6,671 feet (2,033 m)

Difficulty: EASY on gentle inclines.

Surface: Paved black top and some dirt single-track.

Restrooms are available in buildings on the west side of Trailside Park.

NOTABLE FEATURES:

◊   The park offers **sports** fields and courts, **playgrounds**, off-leash **dog-parks**, a one-mile off-leash **dog trail**, picnic areas, and a **skateboard park**. A technical skills **bike park** can provide thrills for spectators as well as cyclists. *basinrecreation.org/parks/trailside*

◊   This walk is **easily combined** with walk #30 Mountain Ranch Estates. Connections to multiple trails including the Round Valley Trail System are accessible from this park. Find maps at *mountaintrails.org* and route directions in *Parking City Hiking Guide*.

DIRECTIONS (ROUTE SUMMARY):

▪   Ride to **bus stop 80150**, *Trailside Elementary on Trailside Dr*. Cross the street to the park.

▪   **Drivers** can access the park by exiting westbound at the Silver Creek interchange on Route 40 to Silver Summit Parkway, or by turning east onto Trailside Drive from Old Ranch Road, just south of Highland Drive. Parking in the lower Trailside Park lot alongside Trailside Drive gives access to several trails. Alternately, Trailside Drive goes south to an upper parking lot, accessible from Silver Summit Parkway.

▪   It's easy to follow the perimeter trails that encircle the venues within the park. The map of this route shows additional trail options.

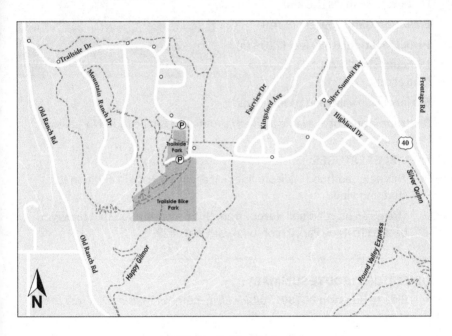

#29 Trailside Park

#30 Mountain Ranch Estates

DESCRIPTION: Traversing one of the premier neighborhoods of the Snyderville Basin, this aptly named loop provides stunning views of mountains, ranches, and estates.

Distance: 2.4 miles (3.8 km)

Elevation Gain: 269 feet (82 m)

Peak Elevation: 6,689 feet (2,039 m)

Difficulty: INTERMEDIATE due to a long ascent.

Surface: Sidewalks and paved roads.

Restrooms are not available along this route but can be found in Trailside Park (Walk #29).

NOTABLE FEATURES:

◊ This neighborhood walk provides excellent **exercise** in addition to stunning **views**.

◊ There's an off-road trail **detour** from this neighborhood that takes you back to Trailside Park to combine with Walk #29.

DIRECTIONS (ROUTE SUMMARY):

- Ride to **bus stop 80180**, *Trailside Elementary on Trailside Dr*. Cross the street.
- **Drivers** may find parking in the lower lot of Trailside Park on Trailside Drive, an east turn off of Old Ranch Road, just south of Highland Drive.
- From parking or the bus stop, walk west on the south side of Trailside Drive. Pass the first corner of Mountain Ranch Drive.
- Turn left at the second corner of Mountain Ranch Drive and follow it around the horseshoe back to Trailside Drive.
- **Drivers** turn right on Trailside Drive to return to Trailside Park. **Bus** stops are across the street to both the left and right.

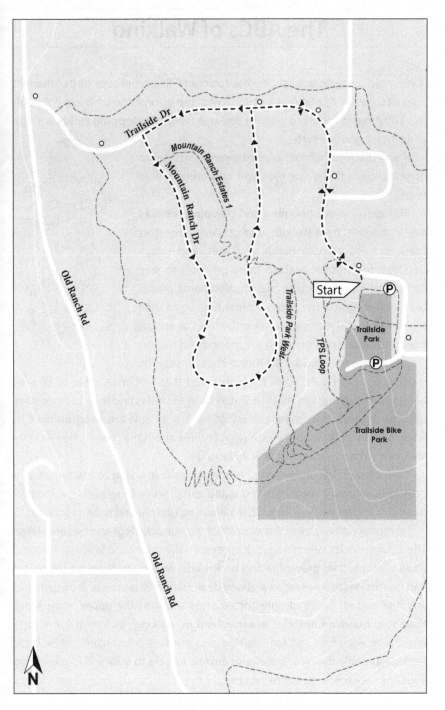

#30 Mountain Ranch Estates

The ABCs of Walking

If you hold a newborn infant by the torso and brush the tops of its little feet against the edge of a table, a foot will try to step up onto the table, even though this baby may not start to walk for a year. A newborn **stepping reflex** is a sign of an intact nervous system.

If you place your finger against a newborn's palms or soles, their fingers or toes will curl around your finger.

Biologists believe **grasping** and **stepping reflexes** are instinctive because our evolutionary ancestors lived in trees. Nimble hands and feet, and shoulders that fully rotate, enabled these primates to step and swing from branch to branch. Newborns probably relied on grasping hands and feet to cling to their mother's fur as she maneuvered in the trees to escape predators attacking from both the ground and the air.

If you've ever watched an infant start to walk by holding onto furniture, you'll have observed that feet know what to do well before the brain masters balance. But as soon as babies find their balance, they become walkers. How remarkable that healthy people are **programmed** to know how **to walk** without ever having to think about the complicated sensory and motor coordination this activity requires.

Conversely, someone recovering from a stroke or trying to master use of a prosthetic leg, may need intense training and practice to relearn how to alternately lift and lower their feet, while balancing upright and moving forward.

In normal walking, all of the muscles of the buttocks, legs and feet are active. The back muscles are engaged to prevent falling forward while contracted abdominal muscles prevent falling backwards. Walking uphill gives the glutes and hamstrings extra exercise; walking downhill increases use of the quads and abs. The natural swing of unrestricted arms activates the upper body. **More than two hundred muscles are involved in walking**, including some forty muscles in each foot and leg. Walking also involves coordination of multiple joints, especially the hips, knees and ankles. Just try to walk without bending your knees or ankles to appreciate this.

There are several differences between walking and running, but the primary distinction is that a **walker always has** at least one **foot on the ground**, while the **runner is briefly airborne** with each step. A race walker would be disqualified from competition if ever airborne during the race.

The difference between "walking" and "hiking" is semantic. Some English-speaking cultures define a hike as a longer-than-typical walk. In American culture, "hiking" has come to mean walking in a natural setting, while "walking" is more often applied to getting around town on foot. Physically, they are the same activity and only the environment is changed.

There are a variety of walking "methods" or purposes, including leisure walking, fitness walking, and race walking. **Race walking** was a major spectator sport in Europe and the USA in the late nineteenth century. Race walking continues to be an Olympic sport, but it is so difficult that even competitive runners rather not participate. **Fitness walking** requires training beyond the scope of this book, but borrowing from fitness walking, here's how to improve the efficiency of **leisure walking**.

Keep **shoulders and neck relaxed**. Avoid the tendency to shrug or keep hands in pockets when it's cold. Hoods, hats, scarves, facemasks and/or gloves are better than scrunching your neck and shoulders.

Let **arms swing naturally** from the shoulders and keep your hands relaxed. You can increase walking speed by increasing the speed of your arm swing but swinging arms too wildly can slow you down. Fitness and race walkers keep elbows flexed about 90 degrees and pump their arms to increase speed and efficiency.

Serious walkers do not carry or wear anything that restricts or burdens the free swing of arms, especially not a shoulder bag. If you walk with a waist or fanny pack that carries water bottles, make sure the width of the pack doesn't have your elbows colliding with the bottles.

Keep your **torso upright**. Leaning backward or forward reduces efficiency. Some people tend to bend forward at the waist when they're **walking up steep hills**, but that's counterintuitive. Gain efficiency and reduce fatigue by keeping your head and torso upright, leaning slightly forward at the ankles, and taking **shorter than normal steps.**

Walk **heel to toe,** avoiding a flatfooted gait. To increase speed push harder with the balls of your feet rather than taking bigger steps. **Bigger steps overwork muscles** and ultimately slow you. **Smaller steps conserve energy**.

Fitness and race walkers allow their **hips to roll** back and forth, creating some twist of the waist. Restricted hip movement impairs speed.

Retro walking (walking backwards) is popular in some parts of Asia. Many people find it restful to walk backwards for a few paces on a long uphill climb. Research suggests that walking backwards may have some musculoskeletal, cardiovascular and cognitive benefits. Besides the issue of needing a rear-view mirror, retro walking in a safe environment may add some variety and fun to your walking routine.

Meditative walking promotes mental and bodily awareness. You could also call this guided imagery, mindful walking, or "woo-woo" walking, but regardless of what you call it, it's worth a try. Here's a sample exercise that you first have to read about in its entirety before doing it.

- To start, stand still with your weight balanced evenly on both feet. With closed eyes, feel the ground. Then connect with your body. Relax your toes, feet, ankles, legs, knees, thighs, hips, and continue up your torso. Relax your abs and your pecs. Relax your gluts and your back muscles. Relax your fingers, hands, wrists, arms, elbows and then shoulders, neck and head. Relax your closed eyes and your mouth, tongue and jaw.

- Feel the air around you and breathe it in.

- With eyes still closed, put one hand on your chest and one on your belly. Inhale in such a way that the hand on your belly rises instead of the hand on your chest. This is called **abdominal breathing,** (a technique used by health care providers for the treatment of hyperventilation, anxiety, and other medical conditions.)

- Still with eyes closed, imagine that the air you have inhaled is energy that becomes a small **ball of light** in your brain and, imagine that you draw the ball of light down through your core into your center of gravity, a little below and behind your navel.

- Focusing on just the ball of light, open your eyes and start walking. Walk at whatever pace is comfortable but walk smoothly to keep the ball of light **balanced in your center**. Extend your head towards to the sky and feel the ground beneath you, keeping your focus on the ball of light. You should feel upright, grounded, centered, and relaxed, except for the energy field surrounding the ball of light. You may feel lighter.

- While you are walking, you'll observe things or beings in your environment. Instead of letting them hijack your thoughts, imagine those beings or things emitting **energy that you can capture with**

your eyes. Draw that energy in with your eyes and draw it down into your ball of light. Feel that energy flow through your moving body.

- Do the same with extraneous thoughts. Use your mind to transform all thoughts, sensations, and observations into energy that fuels the ball of light and the motion of walking.

If a technique such as this is practiced, it can become automatic, enabling the walker to relieve tension and improve mental discipline and awareness of bodily sensation and the environment.

Feet and Footwear: The Walker's Essential Tools

Feet deserve a lot of respect. Those chilly little pancakes at the ends of your legs support a large moving body and whatever other weights you carry. Your feet are the body parts that do the most work, in spite of having flimsy architecture and the least efficient blood supply. Sufferers of foot problems should give their feet the best help available.

FOOT BASICS

If you **walk** across a brown paper bag with wet bare feet, (not just stand on it), your **footprints** should demonstrate your foot type. **Flat feet** (low-arched) make a wide impression, while a **high-arched foot** shows a narrow footprint, Optimal foot structure leaves a parabolic (normal) shaped footprint.

Flat Foot   Normal Foot   High Arch

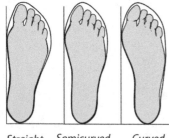

Straight   Semicurved   Curved

The shape of your foot can also be evaluated by holding a straight edge against the big toe joint and seeing how it lines up with your heel. Your foot shape might be straight, semi-curved, or curved. Knowledge of your foot type should guide shoe selection.

A look in the mirror can show your **ankle alignment**, though it is best seen when you walk. Ankles that tilt or roll inward (**pronate**) are common. Less common are ankles that tilt or roll outward (**supinate**). Pronators are commonly called "duck-footed," and supinators are called "pigeon-toed." Some degree of ankle pronation and supination is involved in normal walking. As the foot lands on the heel and rocks on to the forefoot for push-off with the big toe, it rolls from the inside to the outside and then back to the inside.

Pronated   Neutral   Supinated

Young children often look duck-footed when they first start to walk, but this usually self-corrects with maturation. If a youngster's feet don't eventually "straighten out" or the child walks on just their toes, pediatric evaluation is strongly advised.

Sometimes, what appears to be ankle-tilting, results from asymmetry of the bones above the ankle. If you've just looked at your ankles in the mirror, perhaps you noticed that your legs aren't an exact match. **Most people have a minor leg length discrepancy**. One clue is that the waistband of your pants tilts towards your shorter side. Also, when standing, you probably tend to stand on the shorter leg. If you stood up straight on the longer leg, your short leg would dangle. Have an observer look at the backs of your knees to see if the creases line up. Perhaps the creases between the buttocks and the backs of the thighs are at different heights. Putting your hands on your hips while you are standing and then sitting might demonstrate that your hipbones are not the same height.

Did you mirror self-exam also reveal asymmetry of the height of your shoulders? It's **normal for the shoulder of your dominant hand to sit lower** than your other shoulder. That's why straps fall off on that side.

It's also common for the feet to be different in size and shape. Like the differences between the left and right sides of your face, your **feet are unlikely to be symmetrical**. Some people may have to buy custom shoes or two pairs of shoes in different sizes to make one well-fitted pair.

Unless you have a known skeletal deformity such as scoliosis (excessive curvature of the spine), all of your **asymmetry is likely normal**. You don't need evaluation of a leg length discrepancy unless you are experiencing back or pelvic pain, or pain of the joints and muscles of the lower extremity. Those with pain should seek consultation with a health care provider with expertise in musculoskeletal conditions, such as a physiatrist (physical medicine) or sports medicine specialist.

Looking at **well-worn footwear** can also provide information about ankle alignment. People who over-pronate wear out the inside edges of their shoe heels. The body of such shoes might bulge out on the big toe side. Those who over-supinate (also referred to as under-pronation) might see more wear on the heels' outside edges, and shoes may bulge on the little toe side.

Perhaps inspection of well-worn shoes shows that the soles wear out differently on the left and right. That could warrant an **orthotic adjustment** on only one side, while correcting the unaffected side could cause problems. If you have significant asymmetry of your feet, a skilled orthotic technician may be able to correct some problems with customized shoe inserts.

Lastly with regard to your precious feet, keeping **toenails trimmed** is important to shoe fit, footwear longevity, and to avoid trauma to the nails. Toenails should be trimmed straight across, but not too short.

SHOES, SHOELACES AND SOCKS

Before discussing the features of appropriate shoes, I want to make it clear that flip-flops or backless sandals are inappropriate for walking. Such footwear causes you to curl your toes and lift your foot and leg higher than normal, overusing muscles in an unnatural way. Backless shoes also increase the risk of ankle sprains, especially on uneven ground. Barefoot walking is not recommended for any of the walks in this book.

Performance athletic footwear is a multibillion-dollar industry and new shoe designs can be genius or disastrous. Below are some basic principles to go by; but in spite of all I'm going to tell you about the properties of an ideal walking shoe, keep in mind that there is no shoe characteristic more important than fit. The most expensive, lightweight, durable, and most fashionable shoe on the shelf may be inferior to a cheap, ugly shoe that fits you better.

Good **walking shoes** should provide support across the top, bottom, back, and sides of the feet. They should feel stable if you hop or jump. Well-designed walking shoes may have an **ankle collar** (extra padding where the back of the shoe molds around the ankle) or an **Achilles notch** (a cut-out at the top of the back of the shoe to reduce irritation of the Achilles tendon). Most athletic shoes have a **heel counter** (reinforcement of the material in the back of the shoe) for added foot stability.

Shoes designed specifically for walking differ from running shoes. **Walkers need more shoe flexibility at the ball of the foot** for smooth push off. Greater flexibility at the front of the shoe puts less stress on the Achilles tendon. Note in this photo, that the walking shoe on the left bends just behind the toes to facilitate push-off. The striped running shoe on the right flexes less and flexes further back, closer to the arch.

Runners need extra cushioning across the sole of the shoe as they strike the ground with a flat-footed gait and a force two to three times their weight. Walkers strike the ground with their heels and therefore need more cushioning at the heel. Notice the running shoe on the right in this photo has a significant **heel flange** which can decrease walking efficiency. Excessive cushioning in running shoes can also decrease walking efficiency, as can lack of appropriate flexibility.

Some walking shoes have some curve to the profile of their outsole, **(rocker bottom)**, to enhance the heel to toe pattern of a walking step. Rocker bottoms may have some therapeutic value for some types of health issues, but there's also concern that a rocker bottom may impair foot flexibility and balance.

Check the **tread** of the shoe's outsole. Thick tread with deep indentations may provide extra traction for slick terrain. Cushy tread may also be more comfortable and durable for those who walk a lot on concrete. However, an excessively treaded shoe bottom may impede walking efficiency and increase the potential for tripping.

Having said all of that, **most walkers will do fine in a comfortable running shoe**. While design differences may be significant for long distance or competitive race walkers, for most leisure walkers, running shoes that provide good fit, support and comfort are usually adequate and much easier to find.

Athletic shoes have traditionally had three basic designs: cushioning shoes, stability shoes, and motion control shoes. Research supporting these designs is limited and there's ongoing debate amongst runners about the value of "minimalist" shoes, which simulate barefoot running, or drop heel shoes, or other novel designs. It's hard to apply running shoe research to walking because runners tend to have a higher rate of foot problems and injuries than walkers. Unless footwear engineers come up with another theory as to what is truly best, merchants are likely to continue to offer these three designs:

Cushioning shoes provide the best shock absorption but less arch support. They are recommended for people with high arches whose ankles tend to roll out (pigeon-toed).

Stability or **neutral shoes** may help reduce mild pronation (ankles rolling in) by stiffening the midsole (the layer between the outsole and the sock liner or insole.)

Motion Control shoes have stiffer heels and straighter shapes to help with excessive pronation. Some shoes try to correct over-pronation by tilting the foot, using extra padding for the insole, or thicker ridges added to the shoe's bottom. Reducing over-pronation can sometimes alleviate problems like plantar fasciitis or shin splints, but improper tilting can cause or aggravate problems.

CHOOSING SHOES FOR YOUR FOOT TYPE

If your foot type is:	Your likely ankle alignment is:	Possibly your old shoe features are:	New shoes should be:
Wide shape, Low arch, Flat foot, Points out	Over pronation, Ankles roll in, "Duck footed"	Worn out more on the inside heel, shoe body bulges out over the big toe	Motion Control
Parabolic shape, Normal arch, Points ahead	Ankles line up straight, Neutral foot position	Evenly worn shoe bottoms	Stability or Neutral
Narrow shape, High arch, Points in	Under pronation, Ankles roll out, "Pigeon toed"	Worn out more on the outside heel, shoe body bulges out over the little toe	Cushioning

After figuring out what type of shoe you are looking for comes the hard part: finding the right type of shoe that fits well. Seeing a hundred styles of shoes on a store wall can be confusing and intimidating. Although there might be knowledgeable athletic shoe fitters anywhere, you're most likely to find **well-trained shoe technicians** in specialty stores. In Park City, ski boot retailers employ some true foot-fitting experts.

Unfortunately, some dealers are more interested in unloading a slow seller than in helping you find the right kind of shoe for your foot type. You might want to call the store to prearrange an appointment with their best fitter, or, ask around to find a reputable store and invest the time it takes to treat your feet like the important body parts they are.

Here are some **additional shoe shopping guidelines**:

Shop **after a walk** or at the end of the day when your feet are puffier. Wear the same thickness socks you'll walk in. A shoe a half-size bigger than your normal shoe size is desirable, especially for walks in hot weather.

The **shape of a shoe** should look similar to the shape of your foot. Some people have naturally curly feet (metatarsus adductus), and people who tend to supinate may also get a more comfortable fit from a curvier shaped shoe.

Fit is critical. Either too big or too small will cause blisters, calluses or worse. Start try-ons with your bigger or more troubled foot. Try on as many styles as needed to find the ones that truly accommodate your feet. The difference between a shoe that feels okay and one that feels good will be magnified by walking. Never buy shoes that aren't immediately comfortable. Successful **"breaking in" is highly unlikely**.

Be careful not to mistake a "cushy" feeling for good fit. Pay more attention to the way the shoe feels all around the foot than to just how the foot feels at the interface with the floor.

The **toe box** should have enough room to allow the toes to freely wiggle up and down. Toes shouldn't jam against the front of the shoe if you walk down an incline. **The heel should not slip**. Check for heel slip with hopping, jumping or walking up steps.

Although shoe manufacturers engineer gender related features into athletic shoes, some women with wide feet will get a better fit in a "man's shoe" and some men with narrow feet might do better in a "woman's shoe". Finding a good fit for small feet in the children's sneaker department is not difficult but finding a quality shoe is. **Children's athletic shoes** are often designed more for fancy than foot support, although there are pricey exceptions. Parents should consider that children might deny shoe fit problems if they love the style.

Walk back and forth on a **hard surface**; it can feel different than carpet. If you're down to a choice between two styles, walk on a hard surface in each for a few minutes. Wear them around the house for a day if store policy allows return of shoes that haven't been worn outside.

Buy the **lightest shoes** you can. Mesh is lightest and can help alleviate sweaty feet. Waterproof sneakers and hiking boots are also becoming lighter as breathable fabrics evolve.

A **removable insole** that facilitates shoe hygiene and allows adaptation to custom insoles is desirable. Make sure there are no nasty seams, bumps, wrinkles or rough spots inside both shoes, especially if shopping in a discount store. High-end bargains may just have cosmetic flaws or be out of style, but maybe they are **cruel shoes** that someone else hastily bought and returned.

High top shoes can restrict walking motion. They might reduce the risk of ankle sprains on uneven terrain and they can provide added support for weak ankles. However, restricted ankle motion might also impede walking efficiency and balance. Most of the walks in this book are on relatively even terrain that should be navigable with low-top shoes.

Buy the best shoes you can afford. Your shoes work harder than anything else in your wardrobe. An investment in good shoes pays you back in comfort, function, and the durability of your musculoskeletal system.

Always **test new footwear** for short distances before taking a long walk. If new shoes feel wonderful after a few walks and you can, buy a second pair before that style is out of stock. The everyday walker may be less prone to trouble spots if they alternate between a few pairs of shoes.

Shoe inserts (orthotics) such as heel cups or cushions may help heel or arch pain or heel calluses. Heel lifts can sometimes correct leg or pelvic length discrepancy. Custom shoe inserts may relieve pain on the inside of the knee. Arch supports or metatarsal pads may improve forefoot pain that sometimes occurs because the shoe is too stiff or too flexible at the forefoot for your foot structure, or because the midsole is worn out. Double-sided tape can secure shoe inserts, though frequent realignments may be necessary. Wrongly positioned inserts can do more harm than good.

Shoes wear out every 500-600 miles (805-966 km) or so, depending on your weight, gait, walking surfaces, and shoe design. An old shoe might still look good while the midsole is disintegrating and no longer providing needed support. Replaceable insoles allow inspection of the midsole. If one particular area is wearing out, a custom insole or a different shoe design might help. **Worn out shoes can cause increased** knee swing with added **stress to knee** ligaments and the patellar tendon. Replacing worn out shoes may alleviate some problems and prevent others from developing.

Consultation with a health care professional is strongly recommended for persistent or recurring pain of the foot, ankle, leg, knee, hip, pelvis or back during or after walking. Complex foot problems may warrant consultation with specialists in neurology or orthopedics. A podiatrist could help you make decisions about foot problems and footwear if you take your well-worn shoes to a consultation.

How you lace your shoes can impact a variety of shoe and foot issues as demonstrated in this picture. **Strategic lacing** can improve shoe fit, comfort, walking efficiency, and may solve some foot problems. A shoe with a thread-the-noodle lace system, like the sneaker in the lower right-hand corner of this picture, provides more lacing options than does standard eyelet lacing.

Many laces need double knots, or they untie and become a safety issue.

Socks may not be part of everyone's wardrobe, but they should be. They can have major positive or negative impact on your walk and your shoes' fit, comfort, hygiene, and durability. As with shoes, **fit is critical**. Too large or too small can cause friction. Avoid tube socks that do not conform to the shape of the heel. Avoid socks that are tight around the leg and avoid any socks with prominent seams.

Socks should **sit higher** on your leg than the top of your shoes. Low cut socks can turn shoes into ankle-biters and won't provide protection from scratchy plants on trails. Long walkers should choose socks with **extra heel cushioning**.

Avoid wearing worn out socks as thin areas or holes can increase friction or pressure, and those areas are usually at the heel or ball of the foot (metatarsal heads) where you most need cushioning. Looking at some well-worn socks gives additional information about your feet. All **socks** will eventually **"bottom out"** but there may be a remedy for why you get holes in the same place all the time.

Wicking fabrics are best. **Feet are sweaty.** An average size foot has about 200,000 sweat glands that under experimental conditions, can produce almost a quart (liter) of perspiration in a week. No wonder the insides of shoes disintegrate! When the skin of the foot becomes moist, it becomes sticky and stretchy, increasing the risk of skin tears. Cotton socks are not recommended as they tend to absorb sweat, increasing moisture and friction.

Wicking fabrics improve sock function. Wicking is the capacity of a fiber or knit to transport moisture. Acrylics, polyester, and polypropylene are some fabrics that repel instead of absorb water. When these fibers are woven into a network of channels, the channels become capable of capillary action; like thousands of tiny straws, they suck moisture away from the skin.

Socks that are suitable for **cold weather** walking are usually blends of wool and synthetics that have been engineered to increase warmth and reduce moisture and friction. Some people will do better in two thin socks instead of one thicker one.

Avoid wearing new socks for a long walk, if they have not first been washed and tested on a short walk. Sweaty feet sufferers and puddle jumpers may want to bring an extra pair of socks along for a long, hot or potentially rainy walk. Walking in **wet shoes** and **socks** is a great way to **get blisters**.

Compressive socks may help with conditions such as diabetes or peripheral vascular disease. **Compressive hosiery** should be professionally prescribed and fitted by a qualified health care provider.

Other Technology and Gear

Gear possibilities are limitless and always evolving, but the purpose of this book is to make walking uncomplicated, so advice is limited to the following:

Google Earth, at *earth.google.com* allows you to preview all of the walks in Park City, (and the world). Aerial photography enables visualization of roads, trails, and topography. Bus stops and landmarks are labeled. Using the street level view, you can see buildings. The system will plot walking, cycling or driving courses for you. Navigation tools are numerous, and this program has traditionally been free. **Open Street Maps** (*openstreetmap.org*) is also free and good for showing detail. Remember though, any map or satellite image can be outdated due to ongoing changes in roads and trails. Also, trees often obscure trails on aerial photos.

Smart phones provide not only a lifeline for the injured or lost, but maps, a compass, help to identify flowers, birds, etc., and apps for tracking mileage, elevation, calories burned, etc. A smart phone app, *alltrails.com/pro*, enables the lost to find their way home. That's of course when the phone isn't lost or has a low battery; so enjoy your phone but don't rely on it. The wise walker knows where s/he is going ahead of time and carries information as to who to contact in case of an emergency.

The **technologic advancement in textiles** of recent decades is significant. Athletic clothing has become increasingly lightweight, wicking, sun blocking, aerodynamic, and expensive, but discounted brands also benefit from the high-tech engineering. While none of this is necessary for a good walk, wearers of old winter long underwear are missing out on the superior comfort, warmth and function provided by contemporary base layers.

Packs for toting water, this book, or other essentials come in a great variety of styles. **Water bottles** should be carefully selected, and not made of soft plastic, especially when warm temperatures promote leeching of harmful chemicals out of the plastic and into your beverage. Two water bottles, one on each side of a fanny, waist or backpack are better for balance than a single large container.

Writing this book, I was reminded of the story of once famous Grandma Gatewood who walked the 2,168 mile (3,489 km) Appalachian Trail alone in 1955, wearing sneakers and carrying a homemade duffel bag. You do not need special gear or clothing to walk.

Conditioning and Walking
with Health Problems

A walking program requires **zero preconditioning** for healthy persons. Start with short walks and if you have the luxury of time, gradually increase the duration of your walks. Tackle steeper terrain as tolerated. If like most people, your time is limited, work on gradually increasing your walking pace and/or distance with what time you have. Even walking for twenty minutes a few days a week is beneficial. It's now believed that a brisker walking pace correlates with better aging of the brain, but slow walking is still good for you. Park further from your destinations and sneak in a brisk walk whenever possible.

Even for persons who are well conditioned, a walking program should start with an easy pace. Speed and distance should be increased gradually. For most walkers, it takes about five minutes to get the muscles warmed up, longer in cold temperatures. After **warming up**, walking pace may be increased to brisk if conditioning is the walker's primary goal. For those who walk briskly, the pace should be slowed down for about five minutes at the end of the walk to let muscles **cool down**.

As with any unaccustomed exercise, starting to walk can cause **DOMS (Delayed Onset Muscle Soreness.)** That's when it feels great to get out and take a walk on day one, but on day two, the buttocks and/or legs feel achy and tender. With rest, symptoms of DOMS should improve over a few days. Then one can restart walking at a less demanding pace. A physician should be consulted if DOMS is persistent or walking causes pain.

If you are inclined to stretch during or after a walk, bear in mind that **stretching is least likely to cause injury if performed when muscles are warm**, which is why stretching before a walk is not necessarily advisable. Stretching after a walk generally feels good for all those torso muscles that had to contract to keep you upright. The foot, leg, thigh, and gluteal muscles also feel looser if stretched after the walk or a hot shower.

Those walking for leisure may only need to do warm-ups in cold weather and not otherwise worry about these issues. The beauty of walking is the many ways in which it can be done.

Regular walking has been shown to cure some ailments, but even when not curative, appropriate physical exercise can be therapeutic for just about every malady known to man. There is a significant amount of research that demonstrates that the prevention and management of these **27 common human afflictions are all improved by regular walking:**

Insomnia	Asthma
Depression	Emphysema
Anxiety	Low Back Pain
Obesity	Joint Pain
Constipation	Arthritis
Irritable bowel	Osteoporosis
High blood pressure	Migraine headache
High cholesterol	Chronic Fatigue Syndrome
Coronary artery disease (angina)	Fibromyalgia
Congestive heart failure	Alzheimer's disease
Diabetes	Kidney stones
Hypothyroidism	Breast Cancer
Menstrual cramps	Colon Cancer
Susceptibility to colds and viruses	

Think of the human body as a machine. When levers and pulleys stop moving, rust sets in. Even a long car ride can stiffen the knees. Like cats and dogs, some people aren't ready to get out of bed until they instinctively yawn and stretch out their spines, which often spend the night curled up like macaroni. The more time moving parts sit idle, the more the engine will have to strain to start the machine up again. Motion is the oil that keeps the machine functioning. Motion improves bone and muscle strength and lubricates joints by increasing production of joint (synovial) fluid.

In addition to musculoskeletal benefits, walking also exercises the lungs, heart and circulatory system, and improves the function of the gut and endocrine glands. Physicians from Hippocrates to cardiologist Paul Dudley White have professed that **walking is better treatment for many health conditions than any medicine.**

Some medical conditions can be worsened by exercise if performed incorrectly, or with excessive frequency or intensity, and some medical conditions require adaptive measures. Here are some examples:

- Would-be-walkers with heart or lung disease or peripheral vascular disease should first consult their personal physician. Most of the walks in this book are at **altitudes of 6,500-7,500 feet (1,981-2,286 m)** above sea level. The thinner air of these elevations can cause altitude sickness, and/or aggravate symptoms of chest pain or breathing difficulty in persons with coronary artery disease (angina), emphysema (COPD), asthma, anemia, and other conditions that compromise the body's ability to get enough oxygen. **Some persons need to walk at lower altitudes** or may require supplemental oxygen under medical supervision.

- People with **diabetes** should also seek medical advice before beginning a walking program. Regular walking may result in decreased need for insulin, but increased need for foot care.

- Individuals who are very **deconditioned** or who suffer from **neuropathy**, or who have undergone **joint replacement**, may benefit from preconditioning under the supervision of a physical therapist.

- Persons prone to **acid reflux disease** (GERD) may avoid aggravation of symptoms by walking with an empty stomach, or by adjusting their medication schedule.

- People with **allergies** or **asthma** may need to use an antihistamine or bronchodilator before exercising outdoors. Treadmill walking is an alternative on heavy pollen days.

- Individuals who suffer from **chronic fatigue syndrome** or **fibromyalgia**, whose symptoms worsen after exercise, need to embark on a slowly progressive program with built-in recovery periods until tolerance improves.

- Persons with **arthritis** may notice some increased joint pain with the start of an exercise program but ultimately, an appropriate walking routine can improve pain and function.

If you are uncertain as to whether walking is or isn't a good idea with respect to your particular medical condition, consult with your personal health care provider before starting an exercise program. Assistive devices that will benefit some walkers can range from orthotics and custom shoes, to canes, walkers, cane seats, or electric scooters for periods of rest.

Warning: If walking aggravates your medical condition or causes new symptoms, cessation of walking and consultation with a health care provider is strongly recommended.

Don't Become the Walking Wounded

Disclaimer: Information provided in this book should not be used as a substitute for medical advice from a health care professional who has evaluated you. Opinions expressed herein are based on the knowledge and clinical experience of this physician author, who would be the first to tell you that there are always alternative schools of thought on how common health problems should be managed.

Dehydration is a potentially serious condition that can be readily avoided. Many people who visit Park City blame the altitude for symptoms that result

from failure to drink enough water in this high desert climate. Drinking caffeinated or alcoholic beverages that increase water excretion (diuresis, or peeing a lot) can compound inadequate water intake. Walkers who take diuretic medicine (water pills) are also at increased risk for dehydration.

Gradual onset of dehydration causes headache, dizziness, nausea, listlessness, fatigue, constipation and insomnia. Infants and children may show irritability. If dehydration occurs more rapidly, symptoms may include flushing, dry mouth and skin, rapid breathing, rapid heartbeat, and fainting. More severe symptoms include delirium, seizures and heat stroke.

Even though you don't feel like you are perspiring when exercising in Utah's dry air, you are. The **sweat evaporates** on your skin so quickly that you don't notice it. You also lose water through your lungs; that's the moisture in your breath that enables you to see steam when you exhale on a cold day. You won't see the steam in warm weather, but a brisk walk on a hot day can cause significant **respiratory water loss**.

Public drinking water sources are limited and taking water along is advisable for all aged people and dogs, especially for longer walks or any length walk in hot weather. If symptoms of dehydration do not improve with drinking a few glasses of water, **acute mountain sickness** might be the cause, and descending to a lower elevation is therapeutic.

It's possible to drink **too much water**. A long walk in hot weather with only water replacement could deplete the body of sodium, causing a serious condition called hyponatremia or **salt loss**. Symptoms of low sodium resemble symptoms of acute dehydration, except the person doesn't feel thirsty and reports having ingested lots of water. Eating something salty constitutes prevention and emergency treatment, but this is a serious condition, especially risky for the brain. Seek immediate medical attention if hyponatremia is suspected.

Chafing can occur when clothing rubs against skin. Inner thighs and armpits can chafe from the rubbing of body parts. In the dry air of Park City, sweat evaporates quickly leaving salt crystals on the skin. The presence of crystals increases the likelihood of skin becoming irritated.

The risk of chafing is reduced by staying well hydrated and avoiding clothing that is too tight or too loose. Wearing **wicking fabrics** with minimal seams may help. Application of lubricants at waistbands or bra bands, and/or cornstarch applied to sweaty creases is preventive. A variety of lubricants are marketed to athletes for chafing. Even applying some lip balm can help in an emergency.

Blisters occur when there is more acute friction or pressure than the skin can tolerate. The skin responds by making a water cushion between its outer layer (the epidermis) and the underlying dermis where the nerves and blood vessels are. If it's not painful, leave the blister intact, cover it, and fix whatever it is in your shoe that caused it. If it's painful enough to pop, sanitize the area and the pin you pop it with. After the fluid drains, apply an antiseptic and a clean bandage. Clean the skin and change the bandage daily. When it's no longer tender, you can trim away the dead skin that protects the newly growing skin underneath.

Calluses are areas of hardened skin that develop to protect underlying soft tissue from repetitive pressure or friction. **Corns** are calluses with dead tissue in their core. Corns are more painful and may require professional management when over-the-counter remedies don't work. Calluses often occur on the heels, toes and the balls of the feet. They can be asymptomatic or painful. They develop more readily when bony prominences like bunions compress the skin from the inside, or bad shoes cause exterior pressure. Obesity or having long metatarsals or high arches also increases the risk of developing calluses.

If **improved footwear** does not relieve calluses, they are usually controllable by regular filing. Many products are available for this purpose from pumice stones to electric sanders and devices with sharp blades that require great care to safely use. Persons lacking the vision or flexibility to attend to their feet should consider professional pedicures. If routine filing does not effectively manage calluses or they become painful, medical attention is advisable.

Foot wounds from scratches and scrapes to cuts and punctures all deserve prompt attention. There's a **higher risk of infection** for foot wounds than for other body parts because feet work really hard, sensation and circulation are less robust, and people tend to not look at their feet. Additionally, feet live in shoes, the insides of which are not too hygienic. Consider the following advice for the prevention and treatment of foot wounds:

Never continue walking if you become aware of a pebble, shoelace, wrinkled sock, or **something else besides your foot** in your shoe. Even if it means sitting on the ground, **stop walking** and fix the problem.

Walkers should check their feet as part of their bathing routine. People with foot neuropathy or diabetes should check their feet after every walk. Even minor scratches or abrasions should be thoroughly cleansed with soap and water and covered with a clean dressing. Applying an antiseptic gives additional protection. **Keeping skin wounds covered** helps protect from further trauma or infection and **hastens healing.** Wounds should be cleansed, dried, and re-bandaged every day until healed.

Lacerations to the bottom of the feet are concerning because if they heal with scar tissue, foot function can be impaired. Big, deep, jagged or dirty cuts of the soles always warrant professional care. If a foot wound does not heal, appears infected, or is associated with increasing pain, immediate medical attention is recommended. Considering that the foot is comprised of 26 bones, 33 joints, 44 tendons, about 100 ligaments, and many fascial planes, foot infections can quickly become complicated and difficult to treat, even for physicians. **Ulcers** of the feet (wounds that do not heal) require highly specialized care.

Puncture wounds to the bottom of the foot also merit prompt medical attention, especially if the sharp object went through a shoe before entering the skin; and especially if that shoe walked on soil contaminated by industrial or animal waste. If the puncture is deep, scrubbing the surface won't decontaminate it. Such wounds are usually treated with copious irrigation with sterile solutions, and possibly prophylactic antibiotics and a tetanus booster. However, even with proper medical care, puncture wounds can result in bone infection, which usually manifests as pain some weeks after the skin has healed. **Bone infection (osteomyelitis)** is a serious problem that may require long-term intravenous antibiotics and surgical bone debridement (scraping away the infected tissue.)

Ingrown Toenails are an inborn tendency in some unfortunate people whose toenails curl down no matter how carefully they trim them or select footwear. For most people, the nails only grow downward because bad shoes push them that way. Pointy-toed shoes are particularly proficient at pressing on the top and side of the big toe's nail. Cutting nails too short also increases the risk. While ingrown toenail sufferers have traditionally been instructed to cut the nails straight across, there may be some benefit in trimming the nail parabolically, which means allowing the sides of the nail to grow a little longer than the center.

If an ingrowing nail presses deep into soft tissue, it acts like a foreign body, causing inflammation and misery. **Emergency management** calls for wedging a wisp of clean cotton between the tender skin and the sharp edge of the nail. A flat toothpick might also do the job. Soaking the toe in warm water first may help reduce tenderness and soften the nail. It is also less painful to slip the wisp of cotton under the side of the nail than to try to wedge it in by lifting the nail's corner. If elevating the nail does not relieve pain, or if there's drainage, medical attention is needed. Chronically ingrowing toenails may be managed with surgical removal of the nail or the sides of the nail.

The term **"shin splints"** describes pain in the front of the lower legs, usually due to unaccustomed use. The pain typically involves both legs, increases with activity, and improves with rest. Swelling of muscles, tendons and possibly even bones is the cause. It's important to rest long enough for shin splints to adequately heal. This can take weeks, depending on severity, general health, and behavior. Returning to activity too soon can result in stress fractures.

Risk for shin splints is highest in new walkers who are not used to hills, wear inappropriate or worn out shoes, have flat feet, rigid feet, tight heel cords, weak ankles or neuropathy, or who tend to overdo things.

Treatment of shin splints includes avoidance of aggravating activities and footwear and icing the tender areas a few times a day. If pain persists, cold and/or warm packs should be applied, whichever feels better. Alternating warm and cold packs and/or massage may help. Use of anti-inflammatory medication such as ibuprofen or naproxen should be considered if rest and thermal applications are not helpful after a few days. However, these drugs have significant side effects, especially with prolonged use. They also may interfere with healing and should be avoided if possible. Acetaminophen relieves pain without interfering with healing. Persistent shin splints deserve medical evaluation. Prescription orthotics, physical therapy, or cross training may be able to correct leg alignment problems that sometimes cause shin pain.

Foot drop means the foot isn't effectively lifted. When asked to flex the feet towards the shin, the person in this photo can only flex the left foot up. A subtle foot drop might appear as a foot that slaps a bit when walking downhill or leaves a fuzzy footprint in snow. It's easier to see if

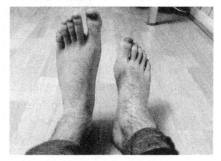

only one side is affected. More severe foot drop results in a high stepping gait in which the foot is lifted by increased flexion of the knee and hip, which wears out other joints.

One of the most common causes of foot drop is having weak stretched-out tendons due to **old ankle sprains**. A bone spur or scar tissue from prior trauma can also restrict ankle joint motion or press on the peroneal nerve that controls the muscles that raise the foot. Foot drop may also be caused by spinal problems that impact nerves to the foot, such as spinal stenosis, disc disease, and/or sciatica. Other conditions that affect the foot nerves include diabetic neuropathy and alcohol related neuropathy. Foot drop due to nerve compression has also been associated with a yoga kneeling exercise, the Varjrasana.

Treatment of foot drop depends on cause. While it's often not curable, an **ankle-foot-orthosis (AFO)**, a device that attaches to the leg and goes inside the shoe helps lift the foot. Untreated, foot drop increases the risk of tripping and sustaining injuries, especially on uneven ground.

Foot pain can have multiple causes and is best evaluated by a physician or podiatrist. Inflammation, stress fractures, ankle instability, over pronation or supination, nerve impingement in the foot, leg or spine, various forms of arthritis, atrophy of the heel fat pad due to aging, steroid injections, circulatory problems, overuse, and/or plain old bad shoes are some of the conditions that can result in foot pain. The heel is especially vulnerable because it supports 110% of a person's weight with each walking step, and 200% of body weight with running. Some heel pain gets better just by inserting a drugstore heel cushion, and some heel pain can be corrected with customized footwear that compensates for alignment problems.

Plantar fasciitis as a cause of heel pain may be difficult to manage, even for health care professionals; but fortunately, it usually improves over a 6 to 12-month period. Pain of the ball of the foot **(metatarsalgia)** or the arch, can also have many different causes and is best managed by a foot specialist.

The big toe is referred to as the **hallux** and disorders of the big joint of the big toe are common, due largely to heredity and bad shoes. **Bunions (hallux varus)**, as seen in this illustration, occur when the big toe bones point in the wrong direction and the joint slowly enlarges, making it difficult to wear shoes.

The term **hallux limitus** means there is a loss of up and down motion of the big toe. This condition can result from repetitive use as in the case of golfers who push off with the big toe to complete their swing, in which case it is referred to as "golfer's toe". It's also been called "turf toe" because it develops after an athlete stubs the toe by catching it on a synthetic field. **Hallus rigidus** is advanced arthritis preventing the big toe joint from being able to bend at all. It's nature's way of fusing the joint to prevent additional damage.

Some people tolerate these hallux conditions without difficulty, while those with intolerable pain or dysfunction may need surgery. **Foot surgery** is a major undertaking that **should be deferred if more conservative options are successful.**

Ankle sprains occur when tendons and ligaments between the leg and foot are stretched or torn. Mis-stepping in a hole or down from a curb are common ways people sprain ankles. Most sprains occur when the foot rolls inward, stretching the outside ankle (**inversion sprain**), but the any aspect of the joint can be sprained, depending on what abnormal position the foot gets caught in. Ankles weakened by previous sprains are at increased risk. Weak ankles may benefit from taping or bracing, while the value of high-top shoes is controversial. Shoes like flip-flops and stiletto heels are excellent ankle "sprainers." Wearing supportive shoes and paying attention to where one walks is the best prevention.

Minor sprains may heal without special treatment. **Sprains that cause immediate pain and swelling indicate significant tissue damage**. If pain is too severe to walk or there's a suspicion of fracture, walking is best avoided. If you had to get out of the road without help, options include crawling or using a belt, scarf, or shoelace to unweight the ankle joint. As illustrated in the accompanying photo, by looping a scarf through the shoelaces and pulling the front of the foot off the ground with hands, walking on the heel may be possible to at least get to a safe place to sit and call for help. Getting the front of the foot up may also help take stress off of the ligaments and tendons. Some practitioners believe that getting the foot flexed upwards immediately after incurring an ankle sprain can reduce initial symptoms and recovery time.

Traditionally, care for ankle sprains has been aimed at reducing swelling by applying ice and compression. While this approach does reduce initial swelling and pain, it may undermine nature's healing process over the long term. The body's natural response to ligament and tendon tears is to increase blood flow to the areas of injury. Blood contains specialized white blood cells that scavenge up the debris of damaged tissue. Increased blood flow also increases the delivery of nutrition and oxygen to the injured structures and carries away waste. Platelets in blood deliver tissue growth factors. About three days after injury, blood brings cells called fibroblasts to the injury. These specialized cells start the repair process by spinning new collagen. Over subsequent weeks, the collagen will be incorporated into the torn tissue fibers to repair them as best the body can. This is similar to the healing process seen in skin wounds.

Icing and compression reduce blood flow to injured tissue, reducing the delivery of the healing elements that blood contains. Taking anti-inflammatory medicine also impairs the body's own natural repair mechanisms, resulting in delayed and incomplete healing. In other words, **inflammation is the first step in the natural healing process**. The short-term gain from stopping inflammation may jeopardize the final outcome.

An alternative approach to **sprained ankle management** includes avoidance of anti-inflammatories, such as aspirin, ibuprofen, naproxen and numerous prescriptions. Whirlpool or massage may be used to enhance circulation, instead of decreasing it. Walking in an air splint with a cane within the realm of tolerance is also advisable. An air splint allows the normal hinging motion of the ankle to keep the joint from stiffening, but prevents sideways motion, which further stresses the stretched tendons and ligaments.

In severely sprained ankles or those not responsive to conservative treatment, imaging may be needed to rule out fracture, or orthopedic consultation may be advisable. For rupture of soft tissue such as the Achilles tendon, surgery may be necessary.

Hand Swelling is a common walker's complaint. I get baloney fingers on long hot walks, but some people complain of their hands and fingers swelling more in cold weather. There are varied theories as to why this occurs, but for most people, it seems to be a harmless condition that resolves within a few hours after the walk. Stretching the arms upward for a half minute periodically throughout the walk or performing arm exercises that keep the arms from constantly hanging down may help prevent hand swelling. Hand swelling that persists for more than two days or is painful requires medical attention.

Bees are essential to agriculture. Most **bees are uninterested in people unless they happen to smell or look like flowers**. Ground nesters, such as yellow jackets, tend to be more aggressive. Avoid wearing perfume, aftershave, shiny bright

jewelry, or clothes with flowers on them. Make sure children haven't dripped sweet juice onto hands or clothing.

If a bee chooses to investigate you, stay still and calm. Some beekeepers believe that bees sense fear, which makes them more defensive or aggressive. Staying relaxed may reduce the risk of stings.

Immediate **management of a bee sting** includes removing the stinger, icing, and taking an antihistamine such as diphenhydramine (Benadryl). It is better to scrape the stinger out of the skin with the edge of a credit card than to pinch and pull it out, as a pinch could cause more venom to be injected. Carry antihistamines and an emergency epinephrine injector system (Epipen) if you have a known bee sting allergy, and seek immediate medical attention, even after using it. The epinephrine in an the autoinjector system is not long acting and more urgent treatment could become necessary very quickly.

Tick-borne diseases such as Lyme disease are starting to trend upward in Utah, though they are still more prevalent in humid parts of the country. In the decades my dogs and I have hiked on Park City trails, I've never seen a tick. However, my little dogs tend to stay out of tall grass, and their smooth coats are easy to inspect. Checking yourself, kids and pets for ticks before getting back in the car or bus may reduce what little risk there is.

Hopefully, you will never need the information in this chapter.

Useful Resources

Notice: URLs for websites and phone numbers may change.

General Info
Park City Chamber of Commerce and Visitor Information Centers
visitparkcity.com

Park City Museum, 528 Main Street, 435.649.7457
and Visitor Center, 1794 Olympic Parkway at Kimball Junction, 435.658.9616

Museums and Libraries
Alf Engen Ski Museum
engenmuseum.org
Olympic Parkway
435.658.4240

Park City Library
parkcitylibrary.org
1255 Park Avenue
435.615.5600

Summit County Library
Kimball Junction Branch
summitcountylibrary.org
1885 Ute Boulevard
435.615.3900

Swaner Preserve and Ecocenter of Utah State University
swanerecocenter.org
1258 Center Drive
435.649.1767

Bus Info
Free Park City Transit System
go.parkcity.org/InfoPoint/ or
parkcity.org/departments/transit-bus
435.615.5301

Trail and Open Space Info
Mountain Trails Foundation
mountaintrails.org
435.649.9619

Winter Trail Information
https://www.parkcity.org/departments/trails-open-space/winter-trails

Summit Land Conservancy
wesaveland.org
435.649.9884

News and Local Info
kpcw radio station
FM 91.7 and on-line
kpcw.org
435.649.9004

The Park Record newspaper
parkrecord.com
435.649.4942

pctv1 television station
Various channels and on-line
parkcity.tv
435.649.0045

Avalanche Information
utahavalanchecenter.org
Recorded avalanche
info: 888.999.4019

Also
National Ability Center
Sports and Recreation
1000 Ability Way
(Quinn's Junction)
discovernac.org
435.649.3991

Image Credits

Pg	Description	Author	License
vii	Photo: Masked person and globe	Anna Shvets	Pexels
3	Photo: Wasatch Mountains	Jesse Gardner	Unsplash
3	Photo: Park City looking west/south	Skyguy414 at English Wikipedia	WikiCommons
5	Photo: Sundance Marquee	Photographing Travis	Flicker WikiCommons
5	Photo: Sound Garden	Nick Calais	Written permission
21	Photo: Salt Lake City Olympic Banner	Tamanoeconomico	WikiCommons
27	Photo: Inversion	Penny Johnson	WikiCommons
104	Photo: La Dee Duh View	Nick Calais	Written permission
136	Illustrations: Step reflex, Footprints, Foot shape, Ankle alignment	Matthew Rue	Purchased artwork
151	Photo: Foot drop	Pagemaker 787	WikiCommons
152	Photo: Bunion	Medical gallery of Blausen Medical 2014	WikiCommons

The author thanks Kenneth M. Hurwitz MD for providing the following images: Front cover photo of McLeod Creek Trail, Back cover photo of the author, Main Street, Ontario Ridge Relic, St. Regis Funicular, McPolin Barn.

The Foot Drop image from *commons.wikimedia.org* with an unknown author is licensed under the Creative Commons Attribution-Share Alike 3.0 Unported license.

Additional *commons.wikimedia.org* images with unknown authors include: Women's suffrage, and Inversion and are licensed under the Creative Commons Attribution-Share Alike 4.0 International license.

Other images from *commonswikimedia.com* are considered to be public domain and include: Mormon covered wagons, Stage coach, Steam engine, Cornish pump, Teddy Roosevelt, and Prohibition raid.

Additional *pexels.com* images include: Girl smelling flowers, Farm stand, and Dog in backpack.

Images from *pixabay.com* include: Walking father/child, Walking women, Hot air balloons, Gondola, Moose, Magpie, Trees, Cairn, Sundog, Cycling family, and Bee.

An image from *goodstockphotos.com* shows Darkly clad figures.

All other photos and illustrations were created by the author.

Acknowledgements

I am most grateful to the citizens and leaders of my adopted home of Park City who've worked so hard to make this beloved town the pedestrian-friendly place it has come to be. Thanks are also extended to the friends and family who supported this endeavor, especially Kenneth Hurwitz M.D., Nancy Costo, Margie Hurwitz, Jodyne Roseman, and Audrey Siegel. Publisher and cartographer Katie Mullaly has made updating of this book a joyful experience. I am also grateful for illustrator Matthew Rue, photographer Nick Calais, and the unnamed photographers who are so generous as to contribute their prized photos to the public domain.

Made in the USA
Las Vegas, NV
13 July 2024

92270033R00095